I0478917

CATITUDE

a Coloring Book of Cats

by

Patricia Burke

**Cover Art Colored
by
DEBBIE CUMMINGS**

ISBN: 978-1-951576-03-5

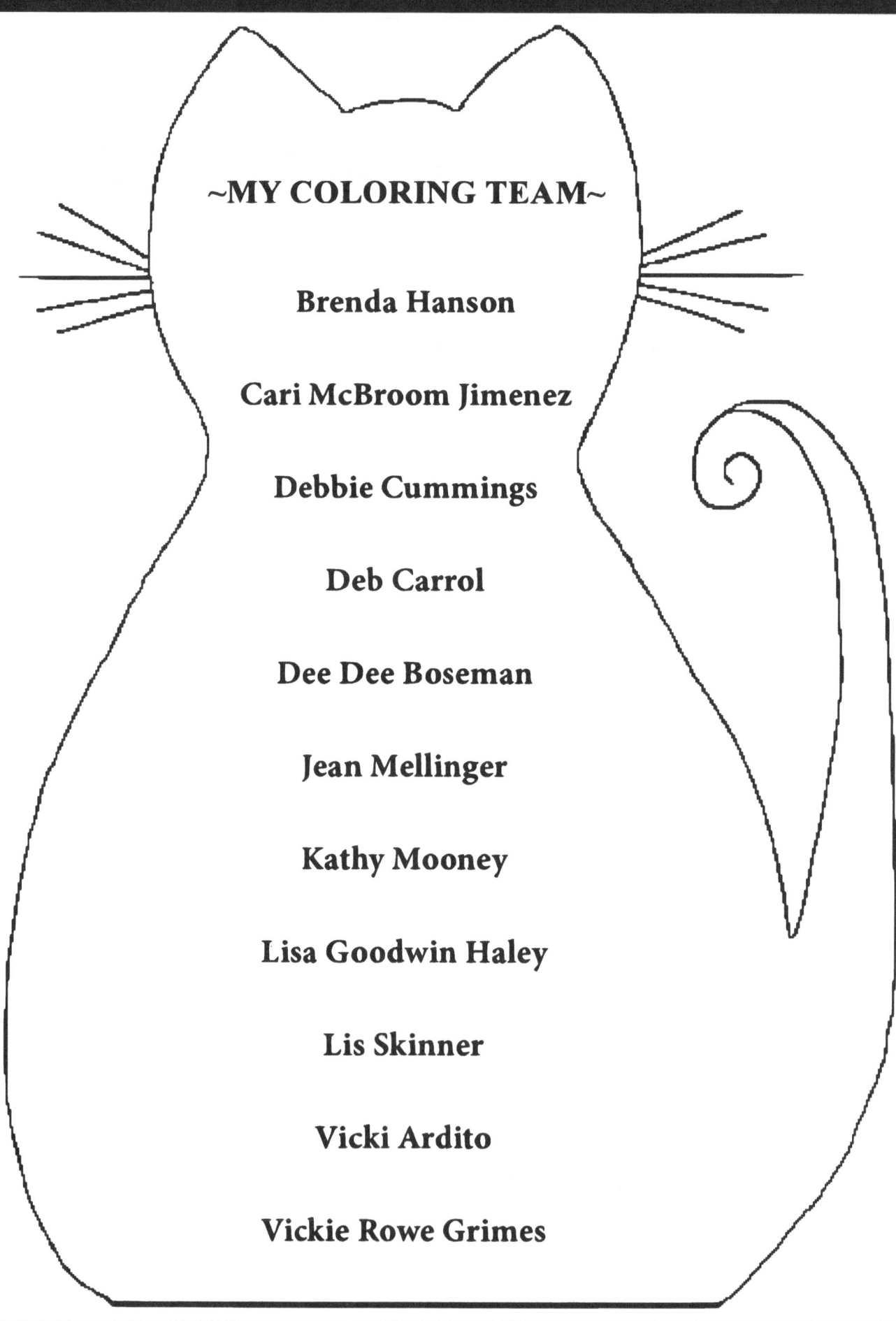

~MY COLORING TEAM~

Brenda Hanson

Cari McBroom Jimenez

Debbie Cummings

Deb Carrol

Dee Dee Boseman

Jean Mellinger

Kathy Mooney

Lisa Goodwin Haley

Lis Skinner

Vicki Ardito

Vickie Rowe Grimes

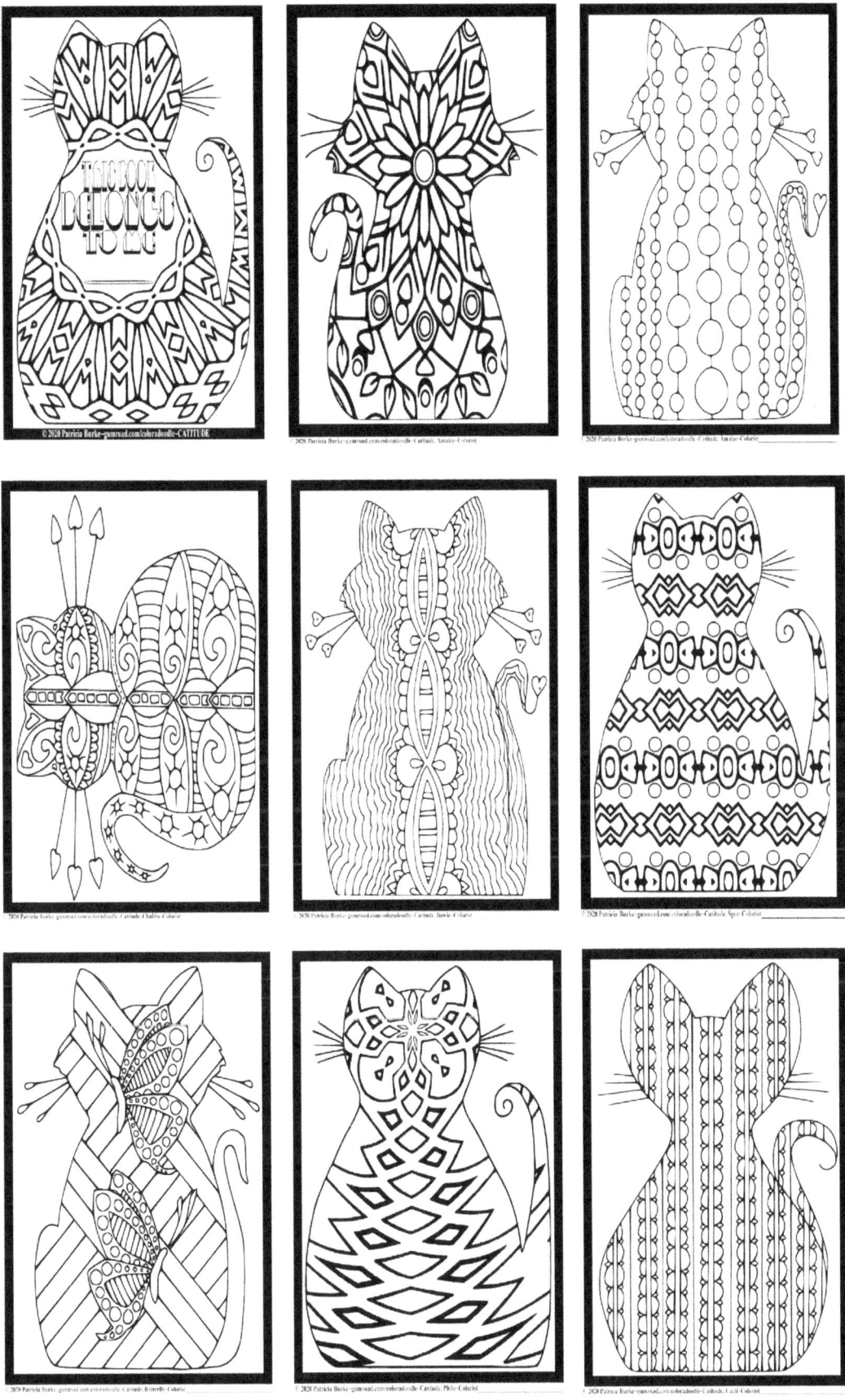

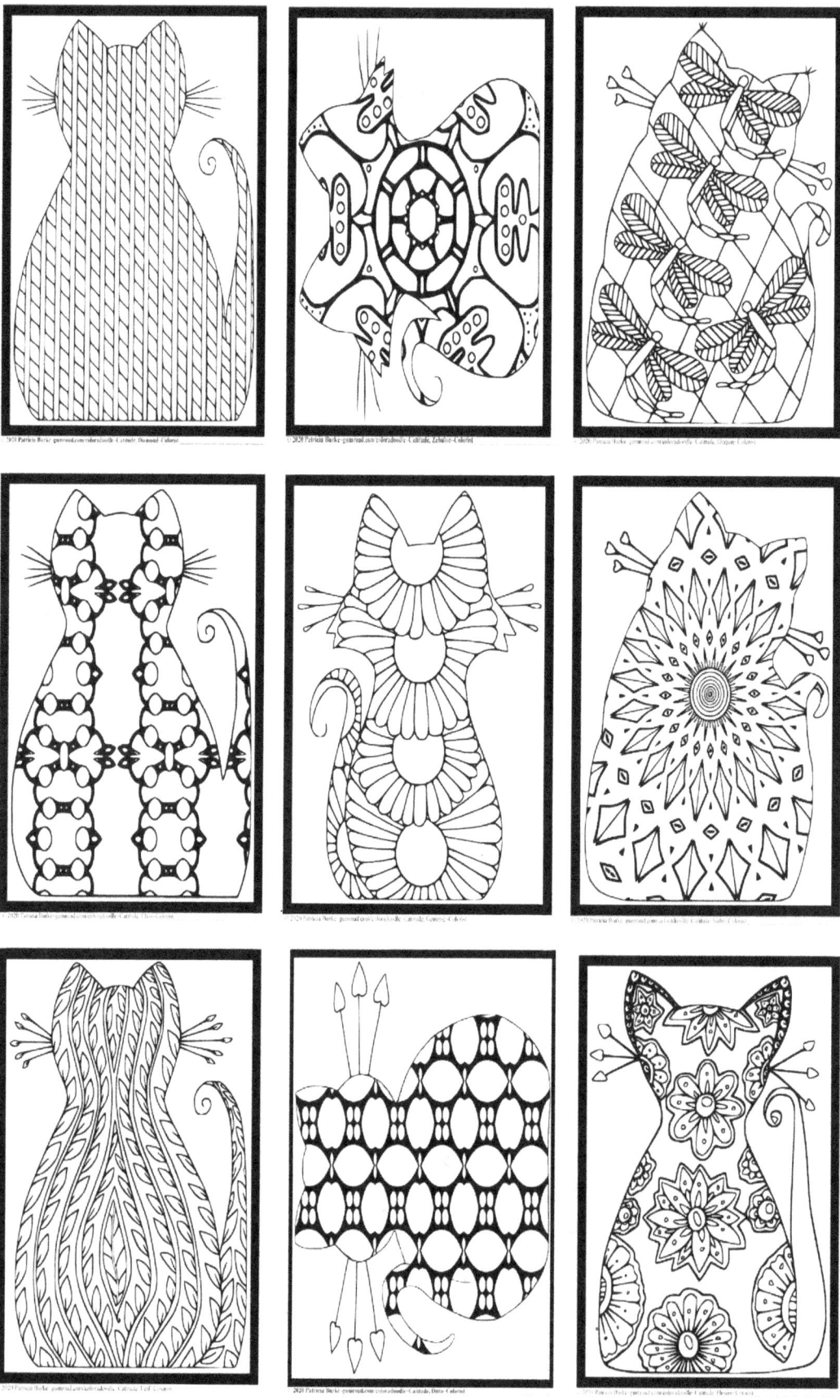

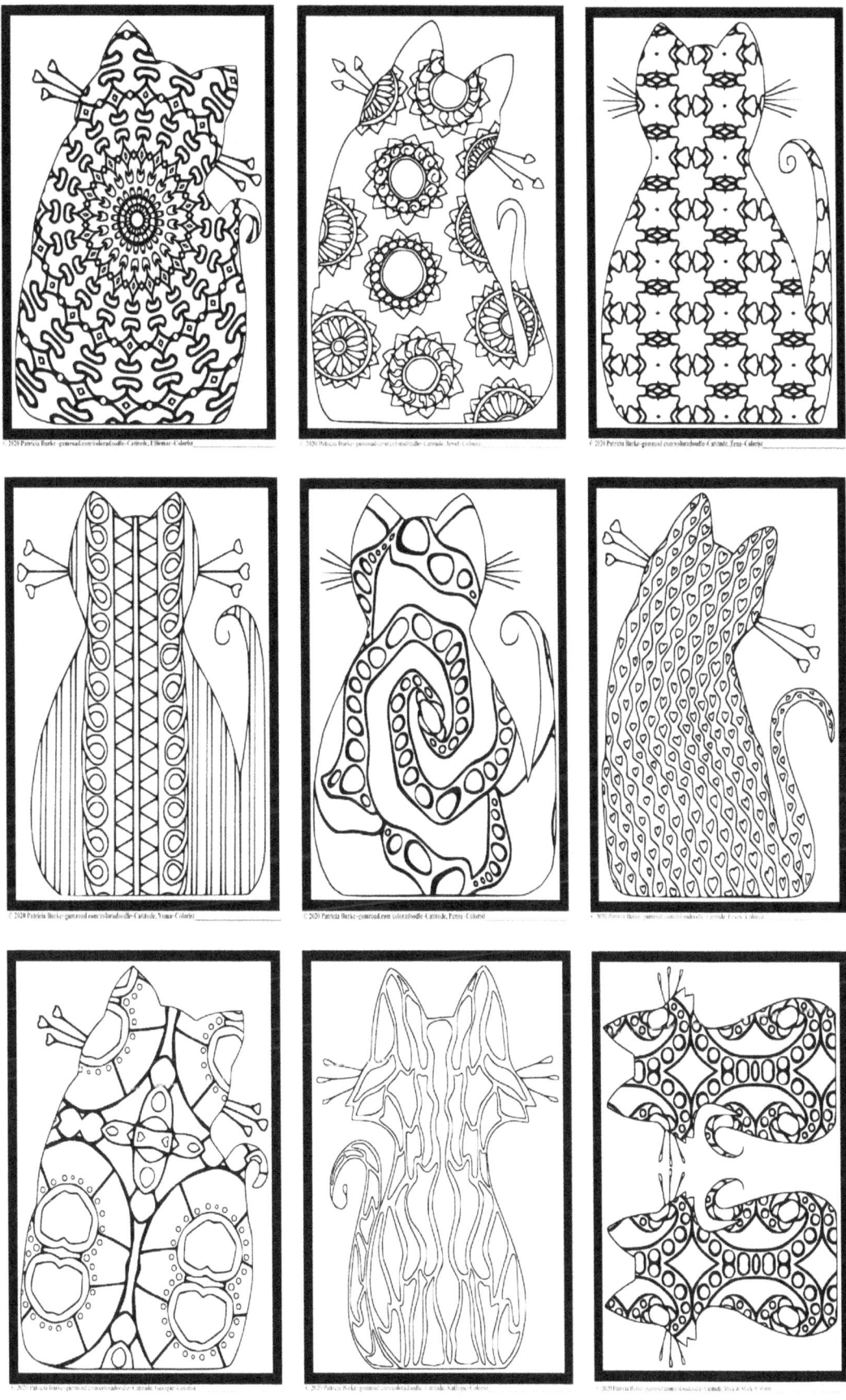

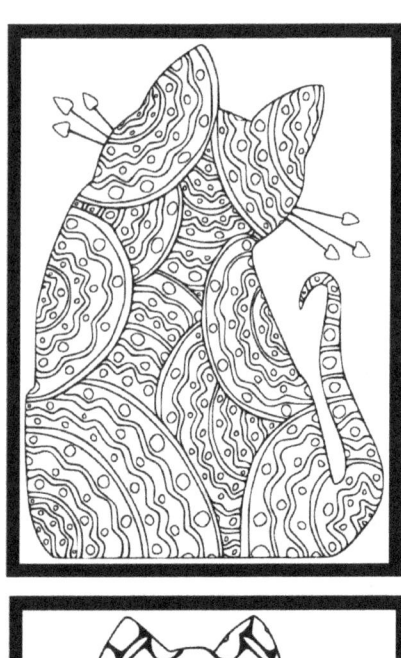

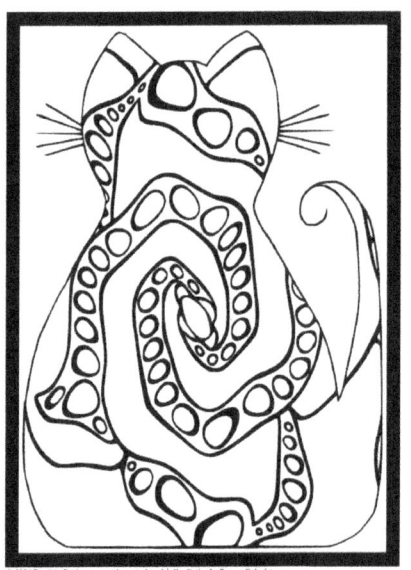

© 2020 Patricia Burke~gumroad.com/coloradoodle~Catitude, Banna~Colorist

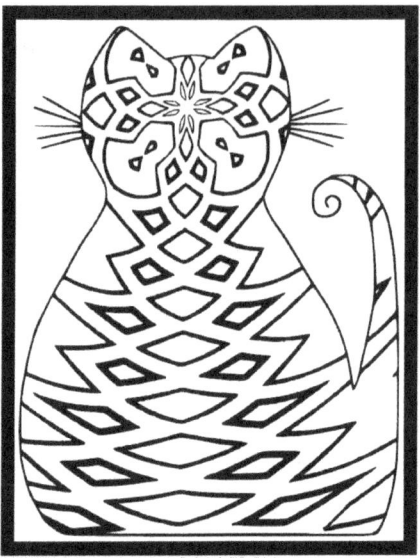

© 2020 Patricia Burke~gumroad.com/coloradoodle~Catitude, Philo~Colorist

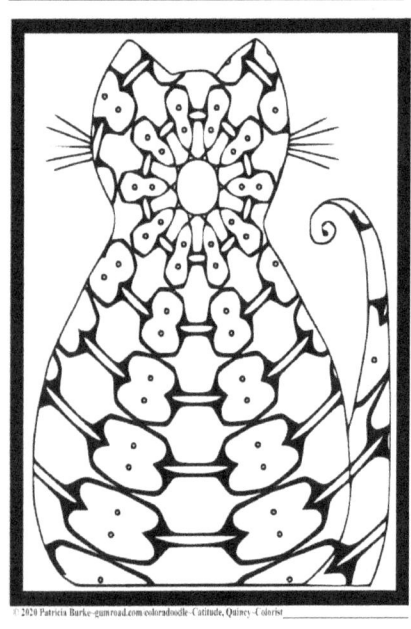

© 2020 Patricia Burke~gumroad.com/coloradoodle~Catitude, Quincy~Colorist

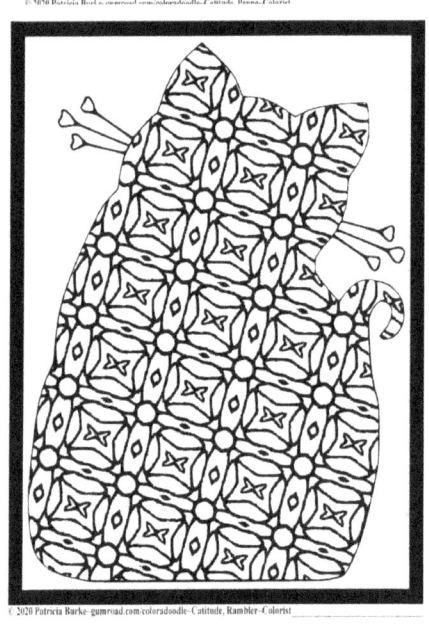

© 2020 Patricia Burke~gumroad.com/coloradoodle~Catitude, Rambler~Colorist

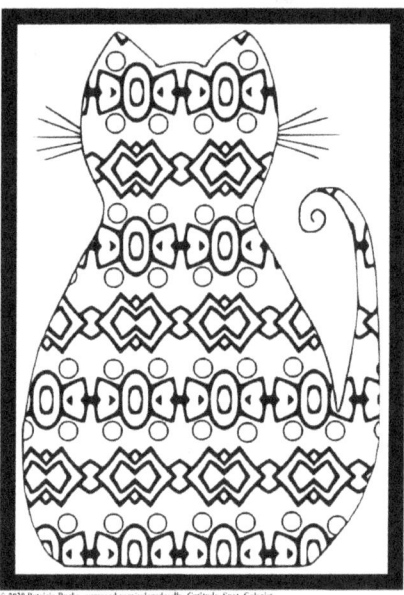

© 2020 Patricia Burke~gumroad.com/coloradoodle~Catitude, Spot~Colorist

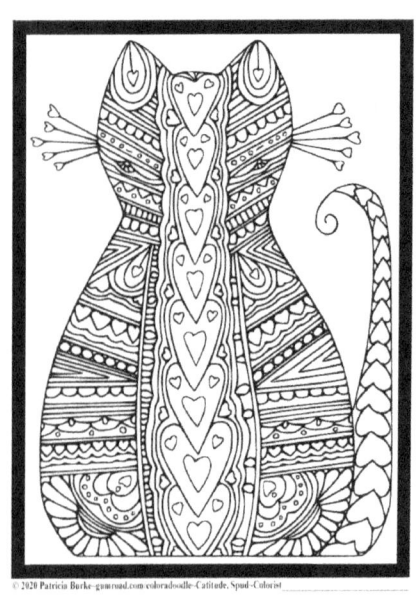

© 2020 Patricia Burke~gumroad.com/coloradoodle~Catitude, Spud~Colorist

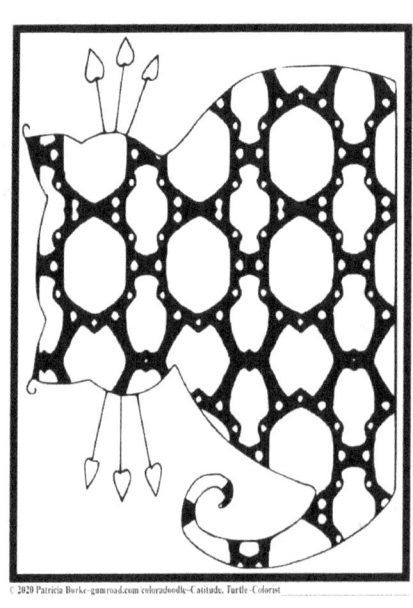

© 2020 Patricia Burke~gumroad.com/coloradoodle~Catitude, Turtle~Colorist

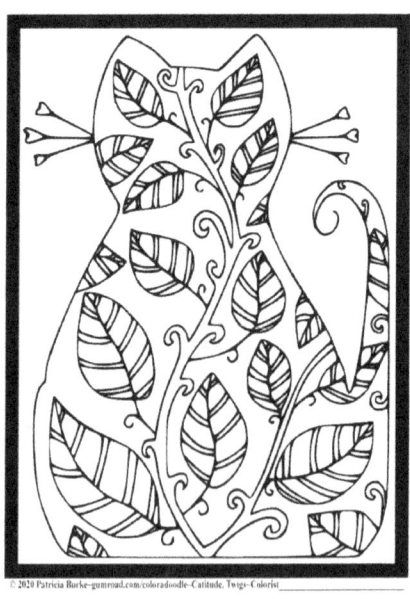

© 2020 Patricia Burke~gumroad.com/coloradoodle~Catitude, Twigs~Colorist

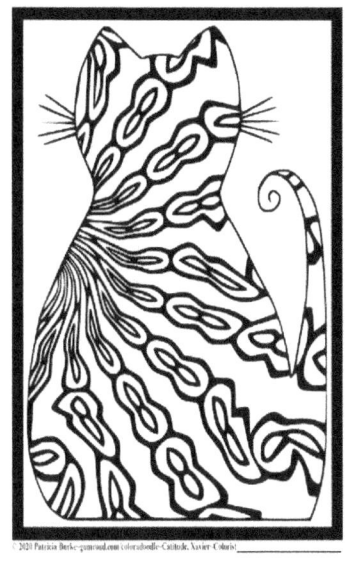

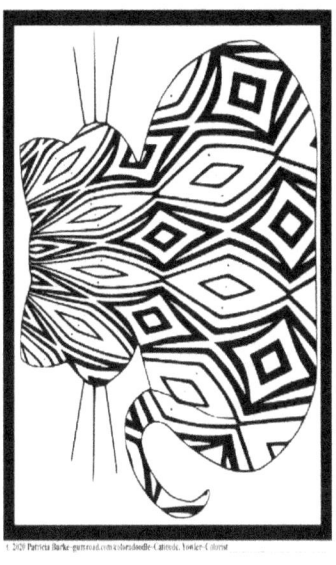

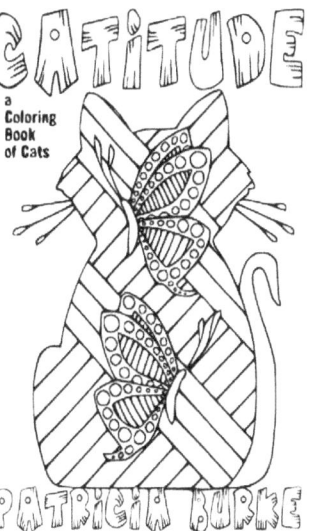

CATITUDE

a
Coloring
Book
of Cats

PATRICIA BURKE

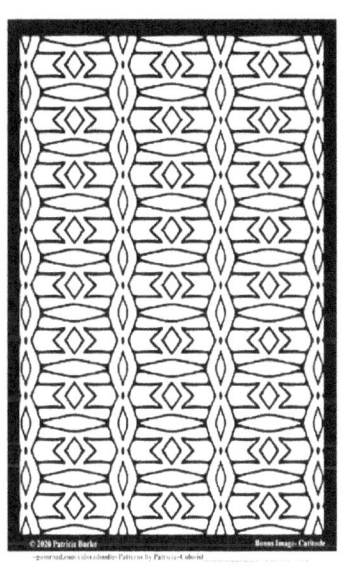

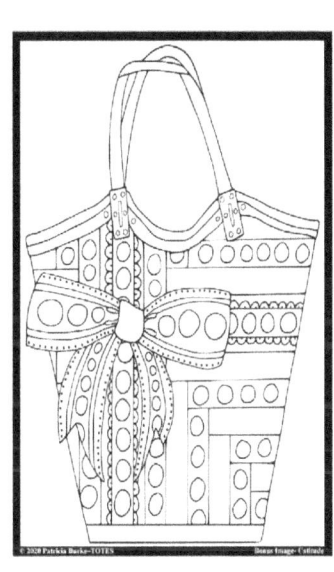

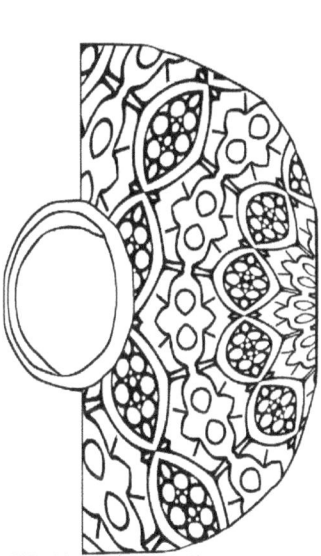

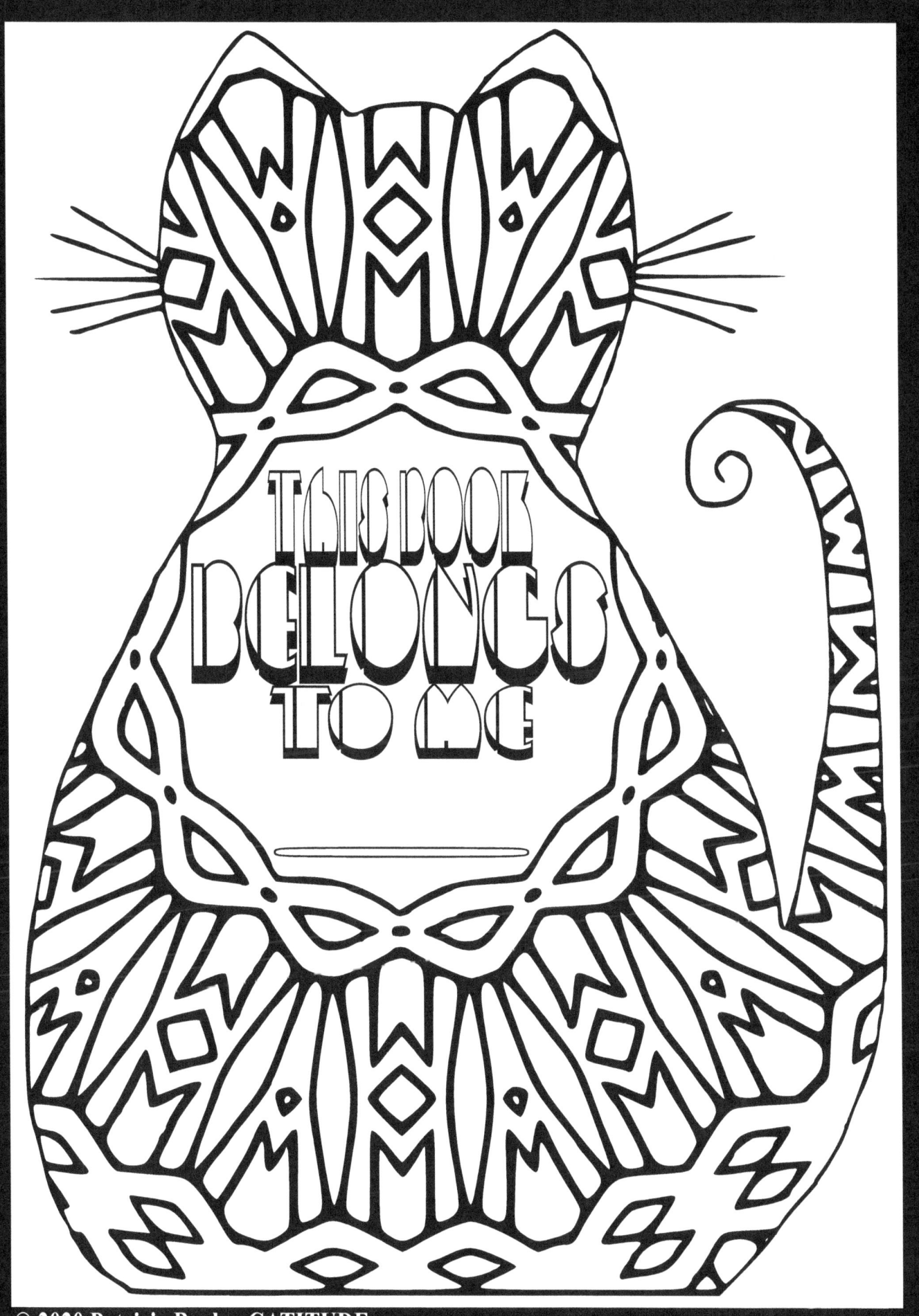

THIS BOOK
BELONGS
TO ME

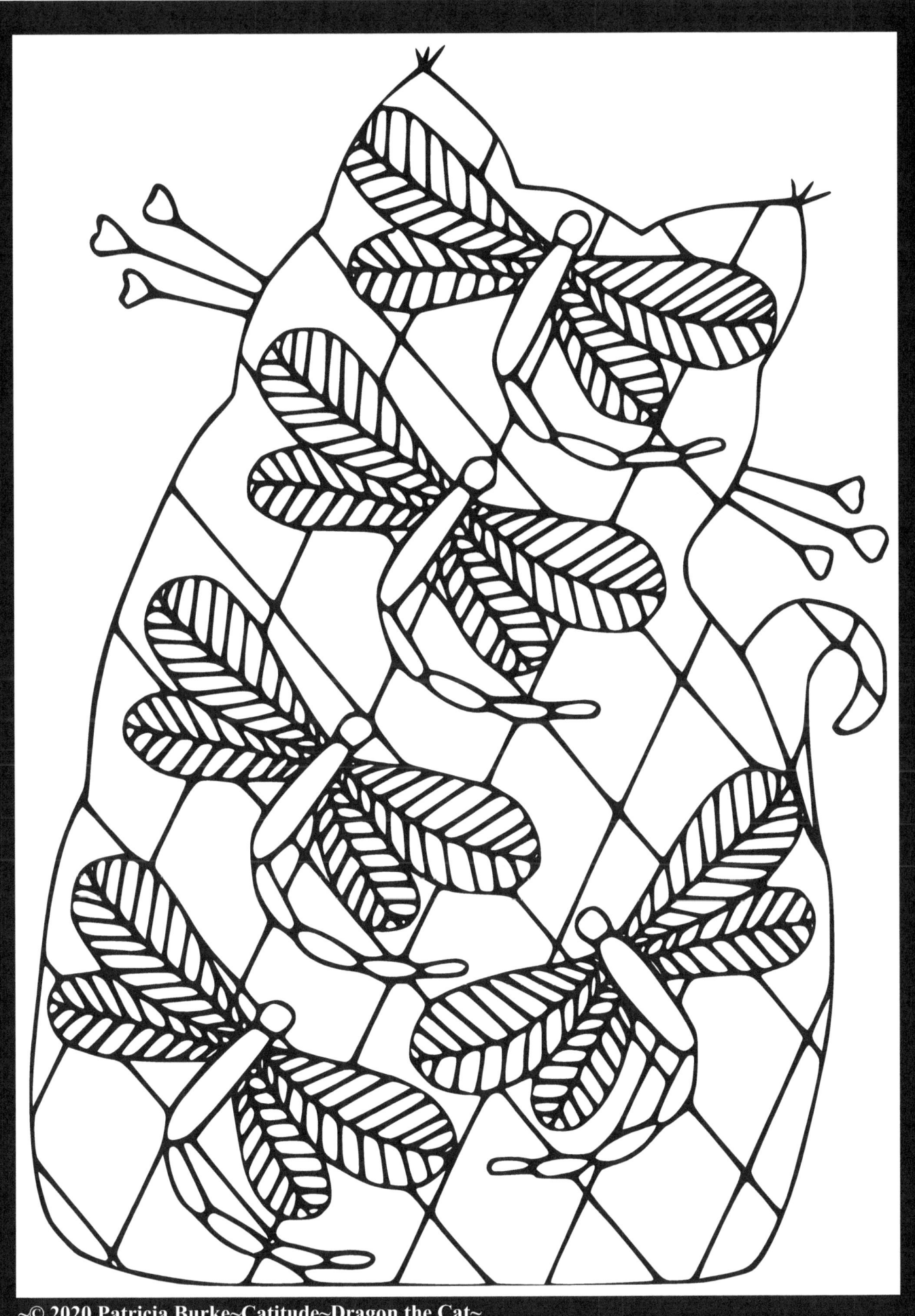

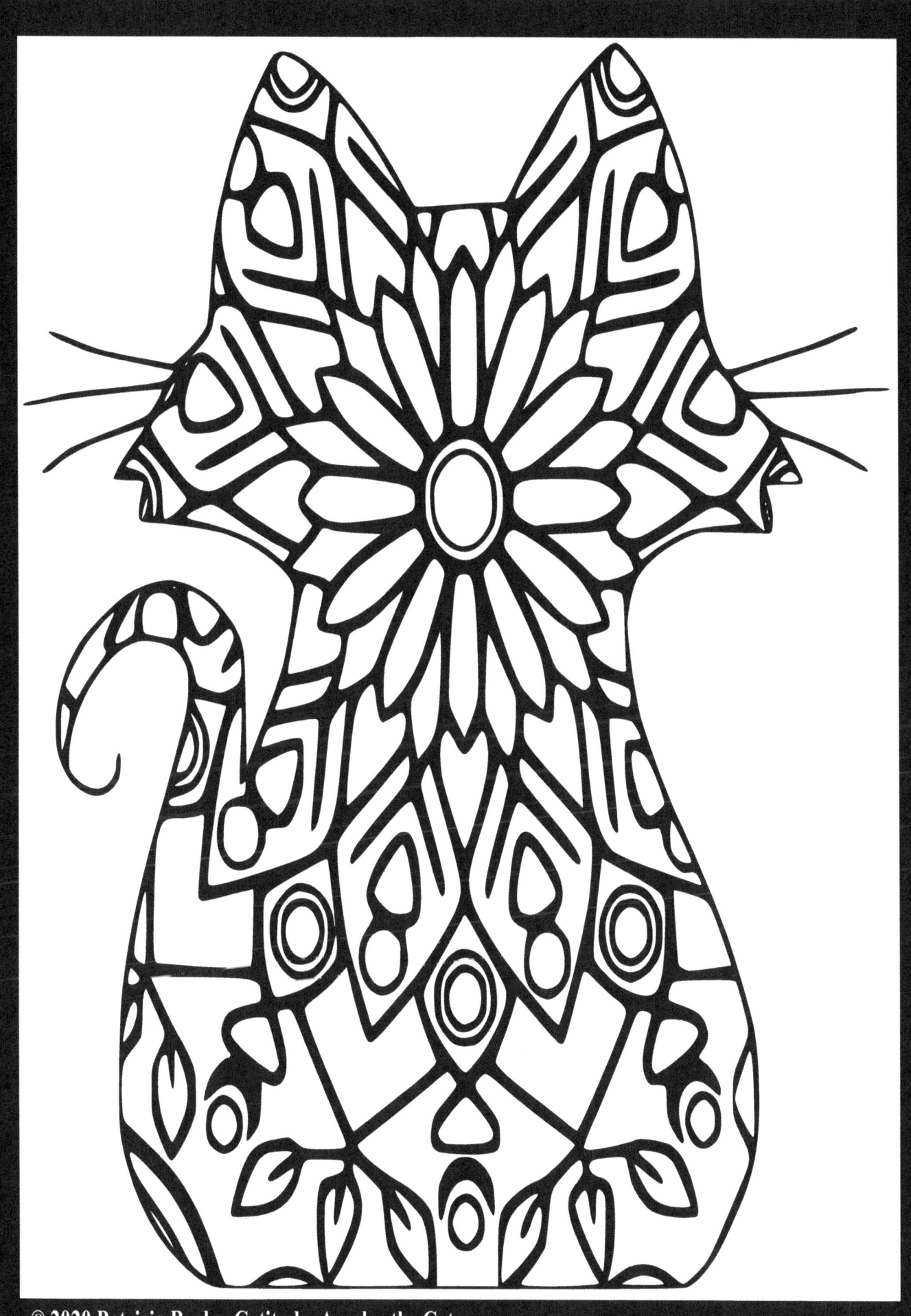

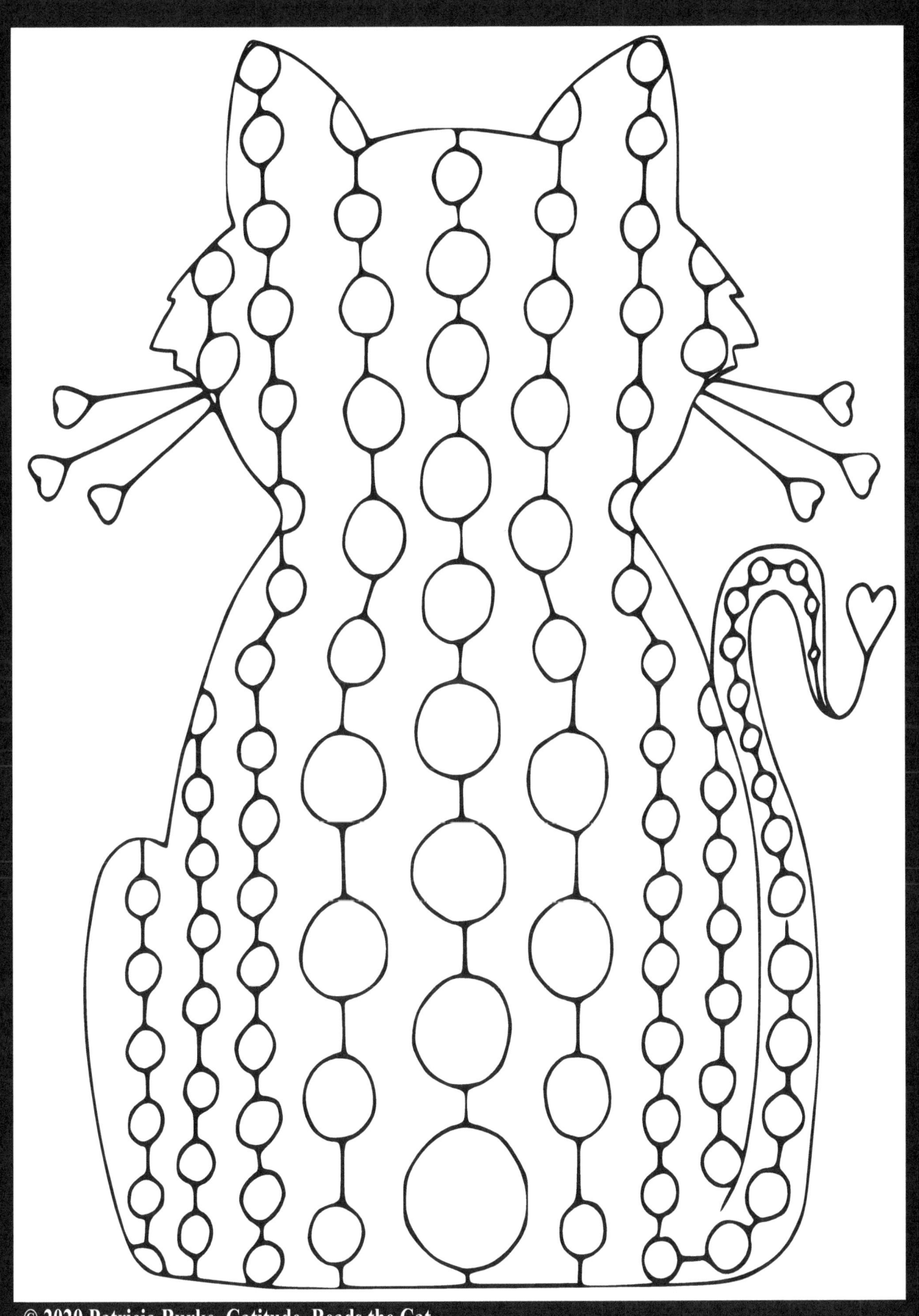

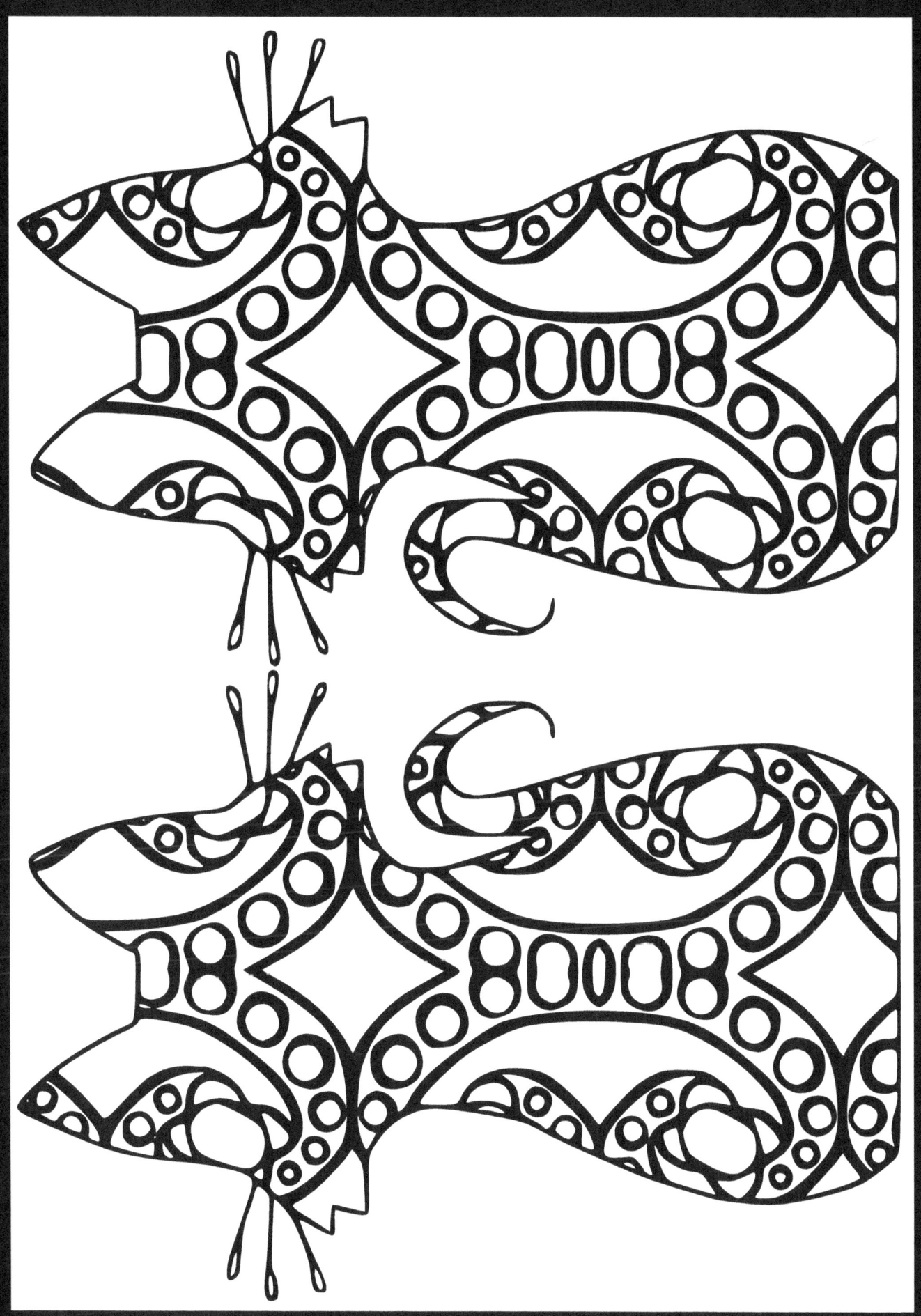

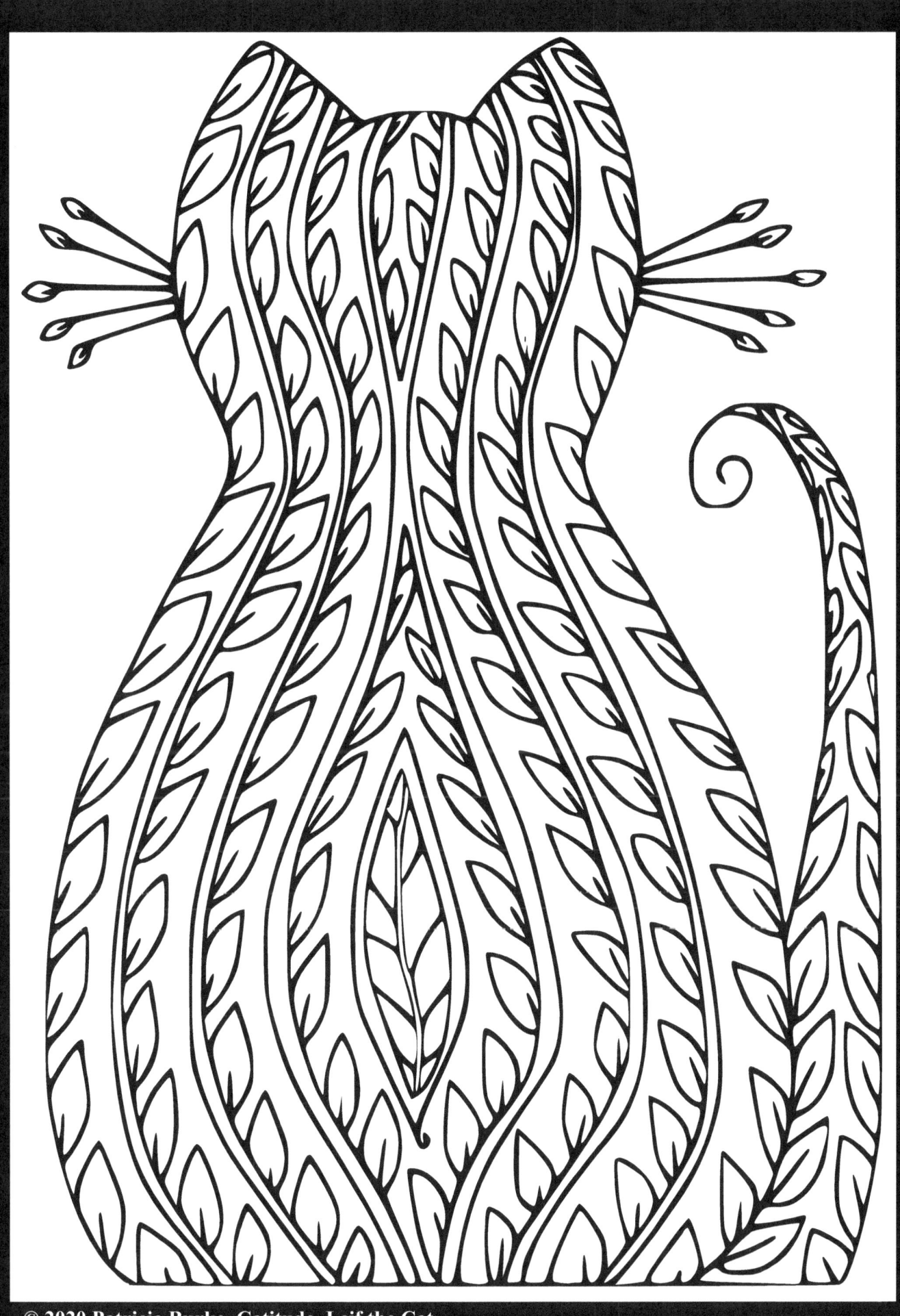

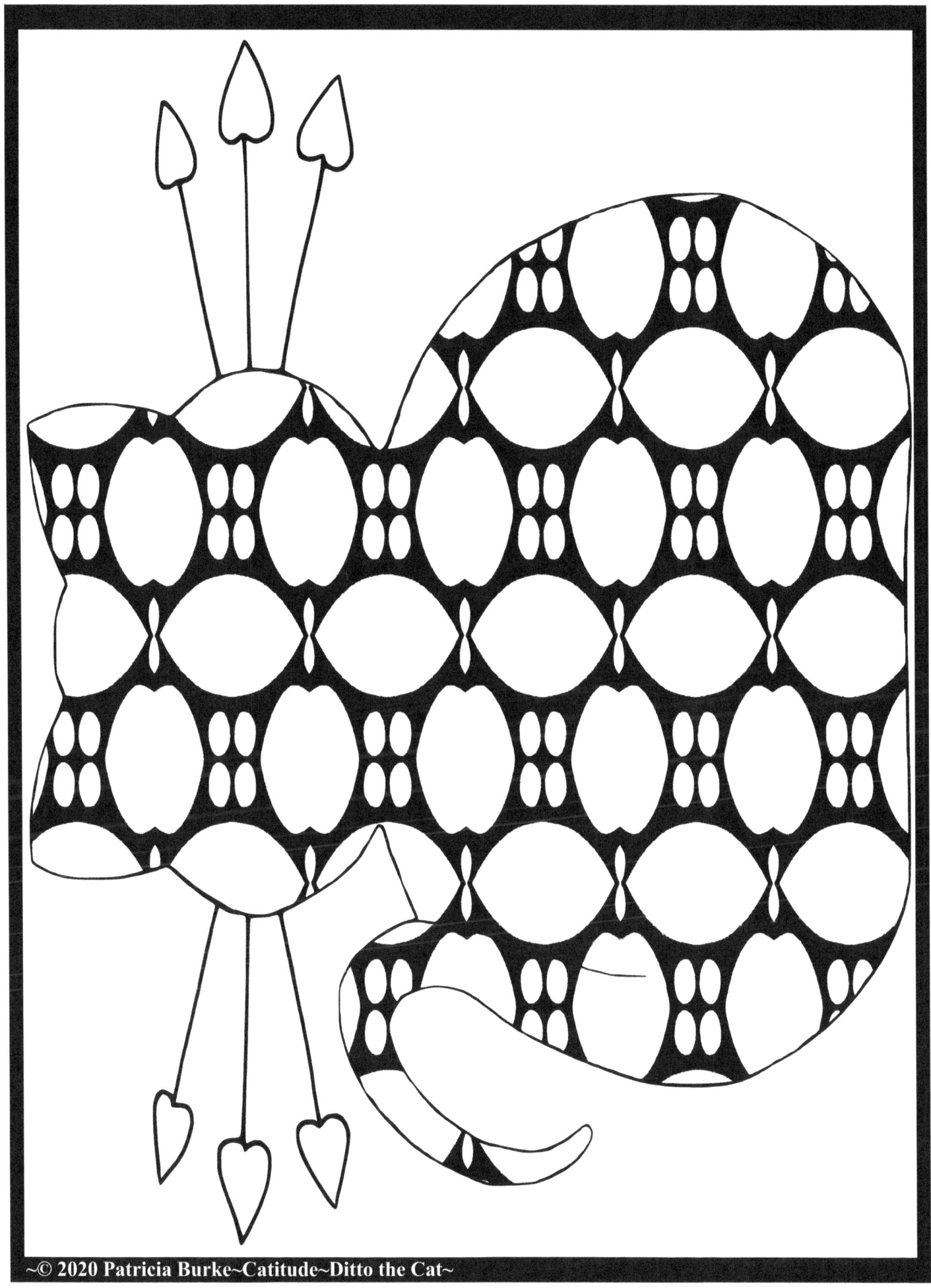

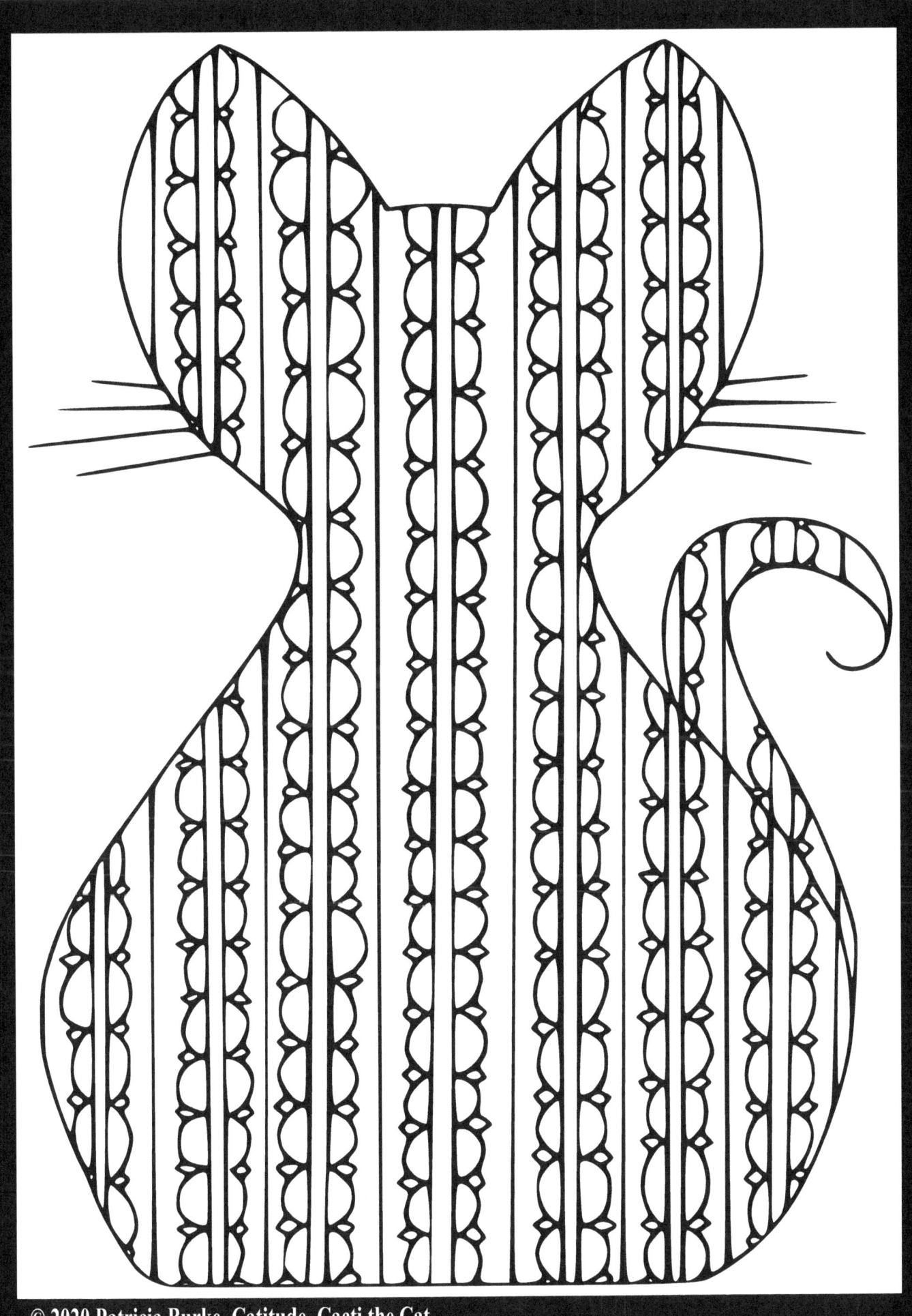

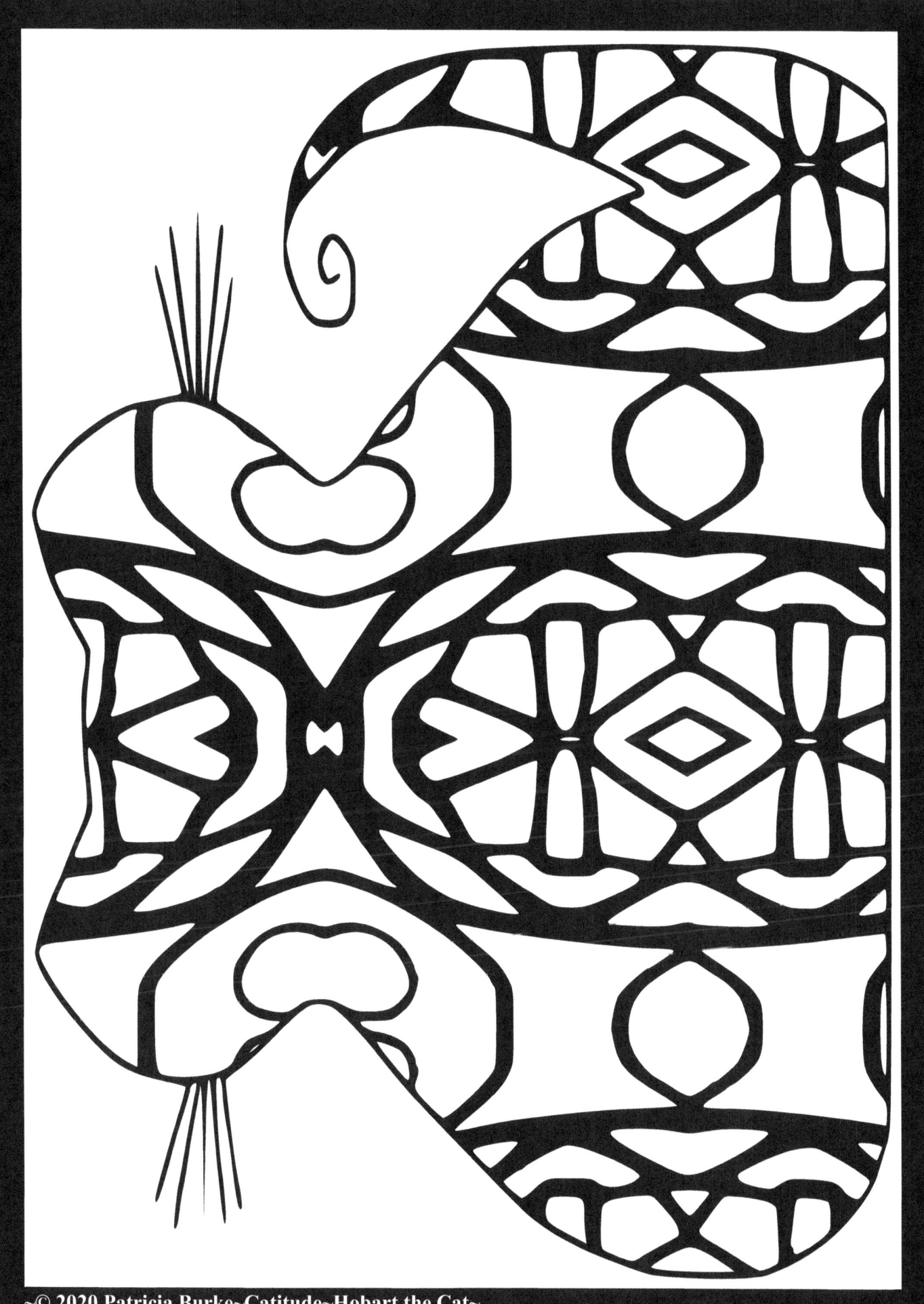

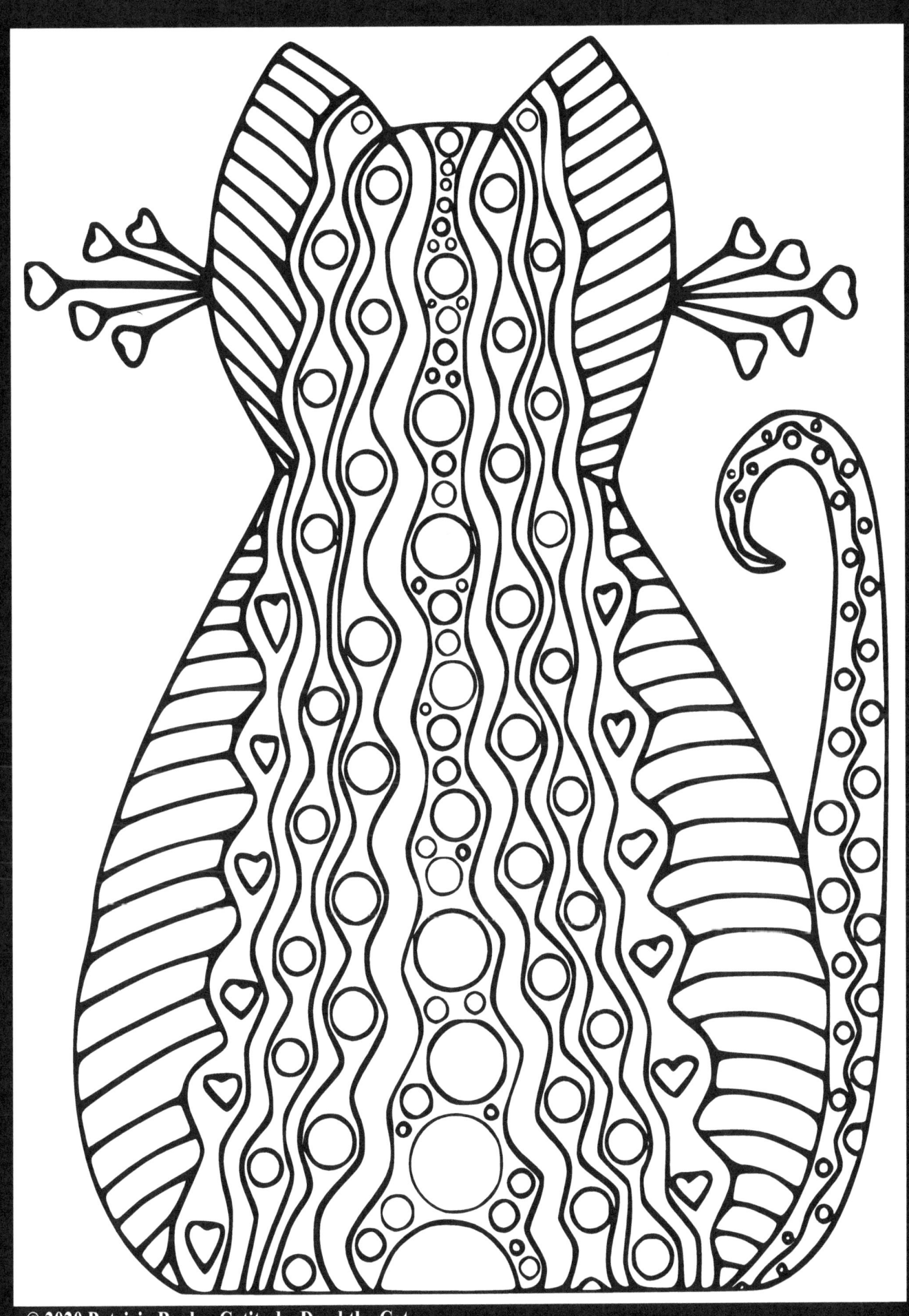

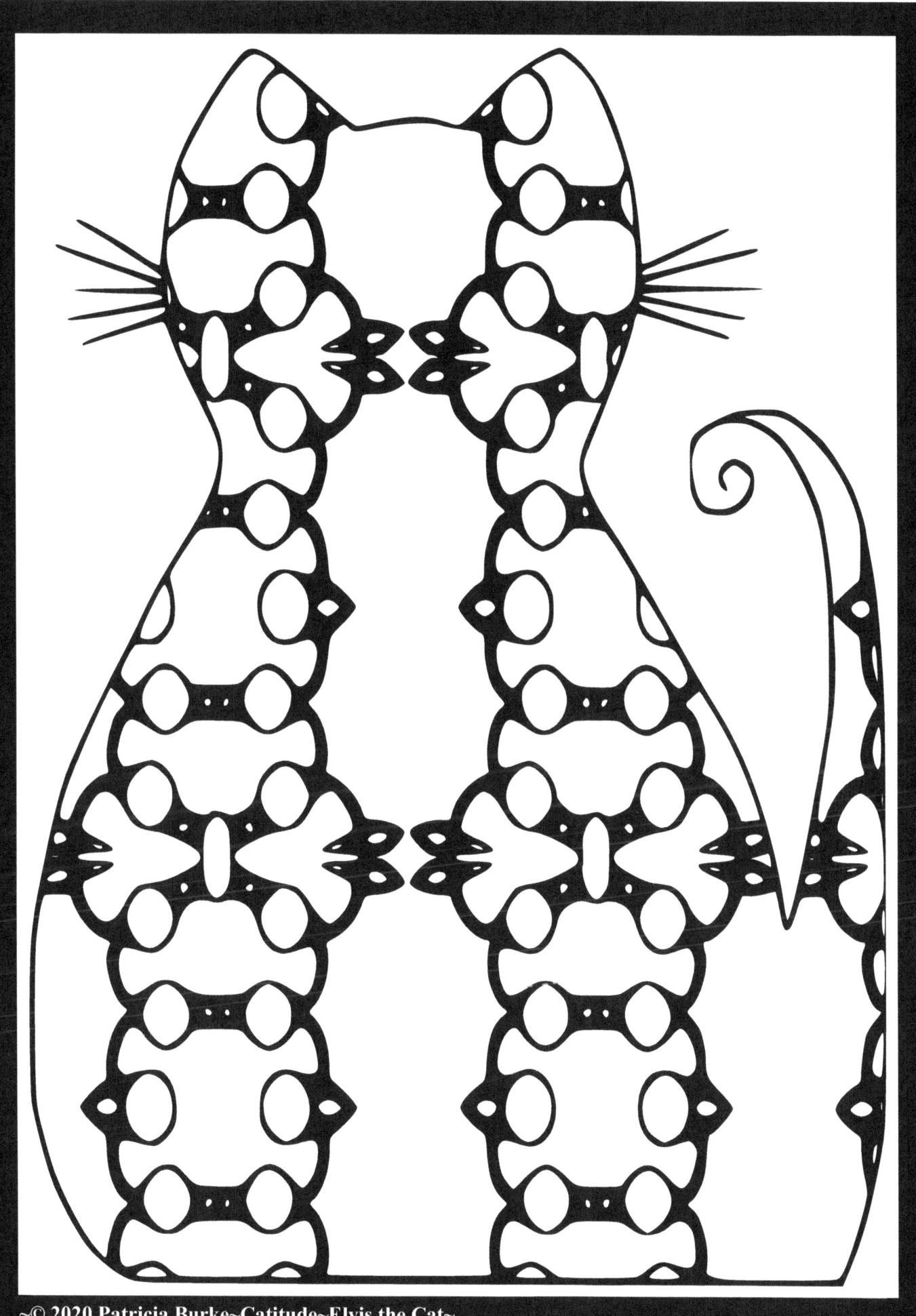

~© 2020 Patricia Burke~Catitude~Elvis the Cat~

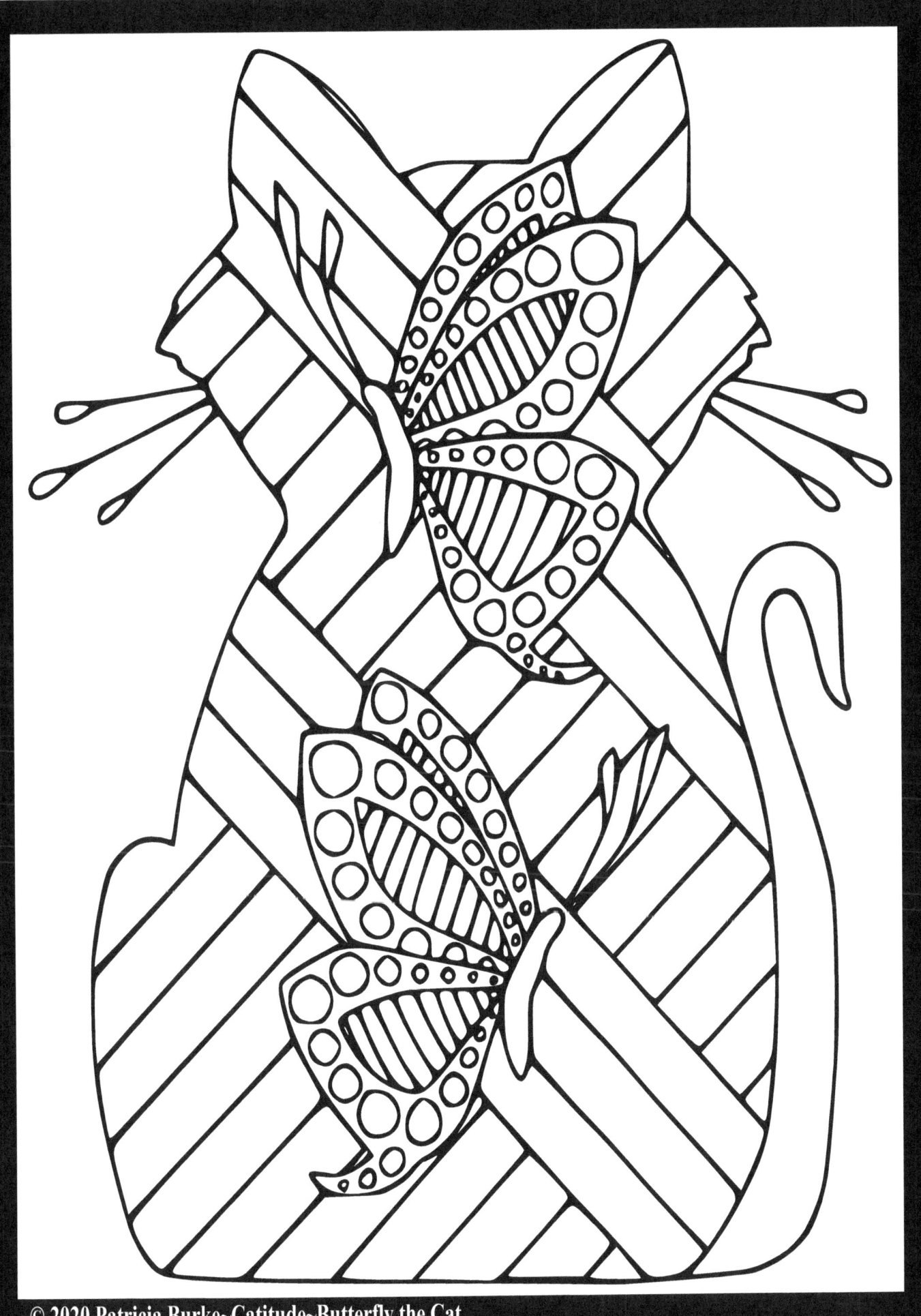

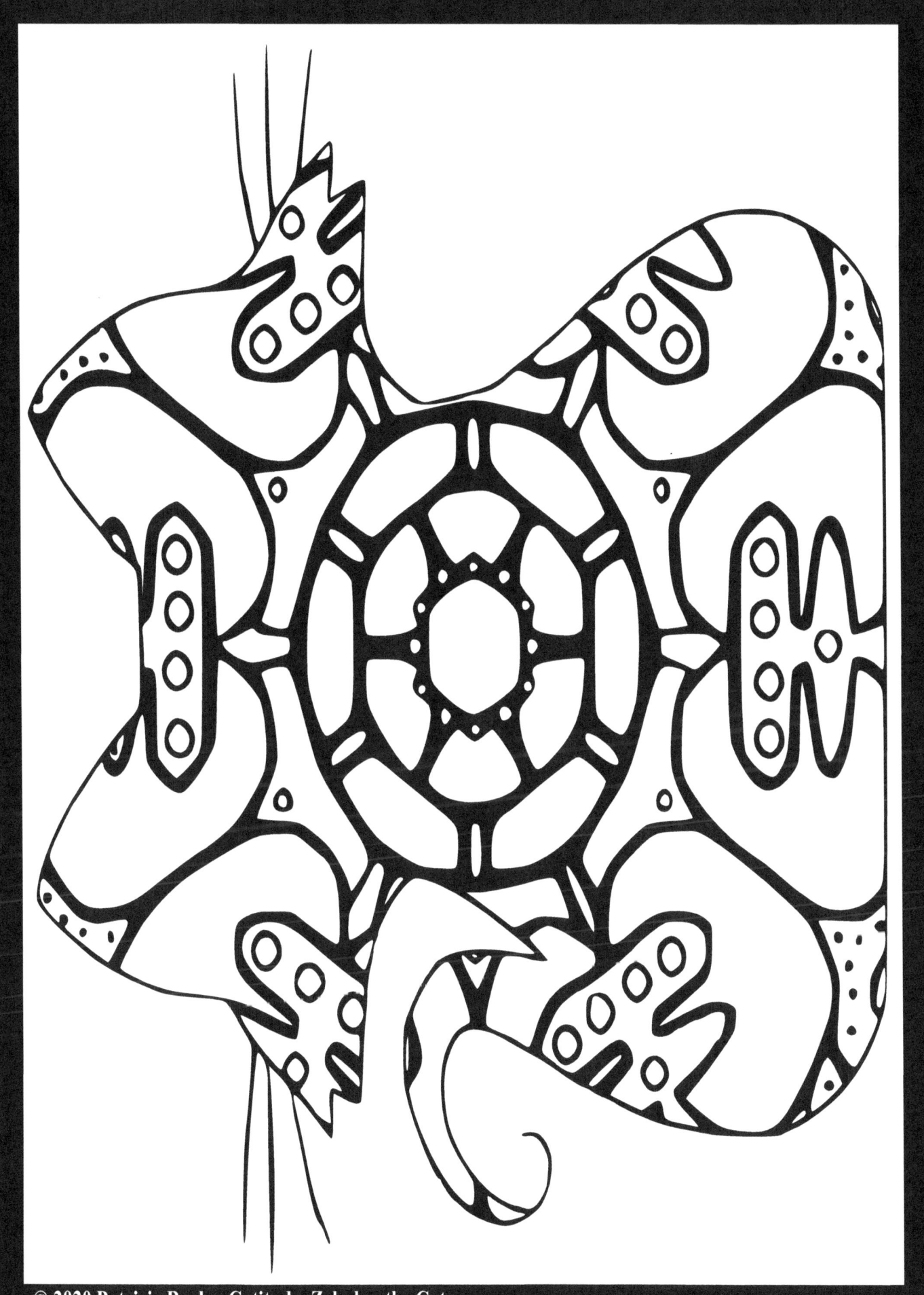

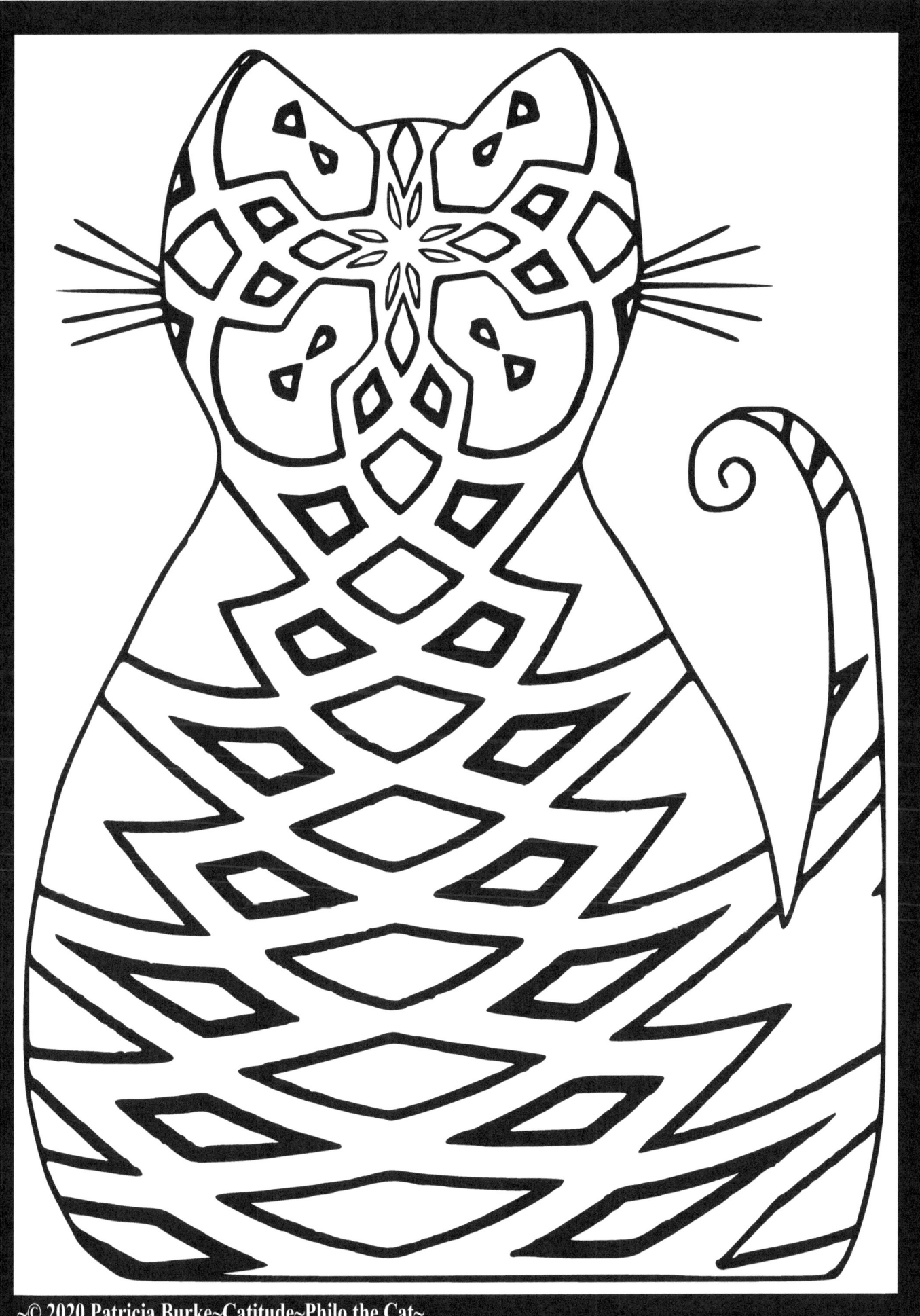

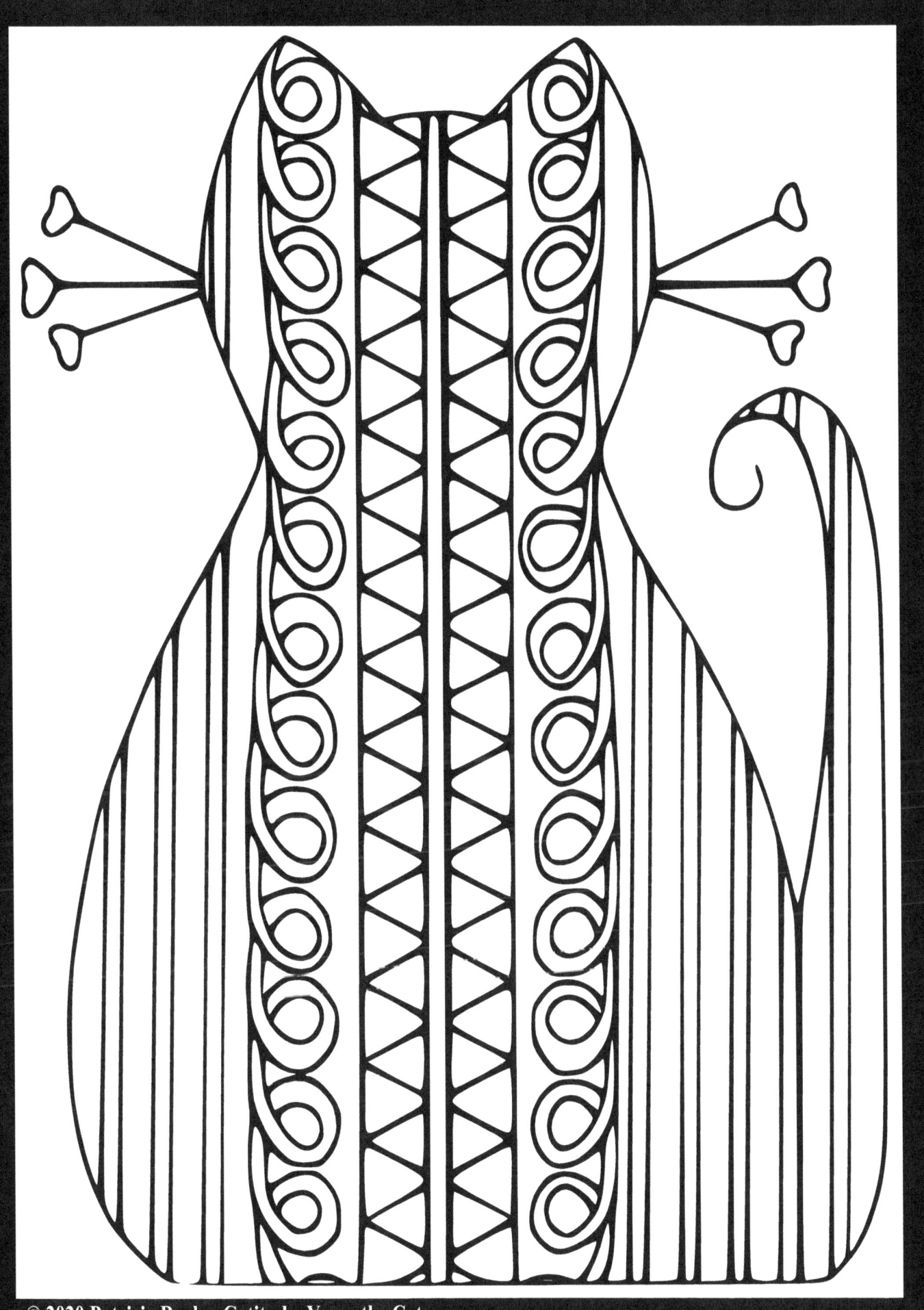

~© 2020 Patricia Burke~Catitude~Yuma the Cat~

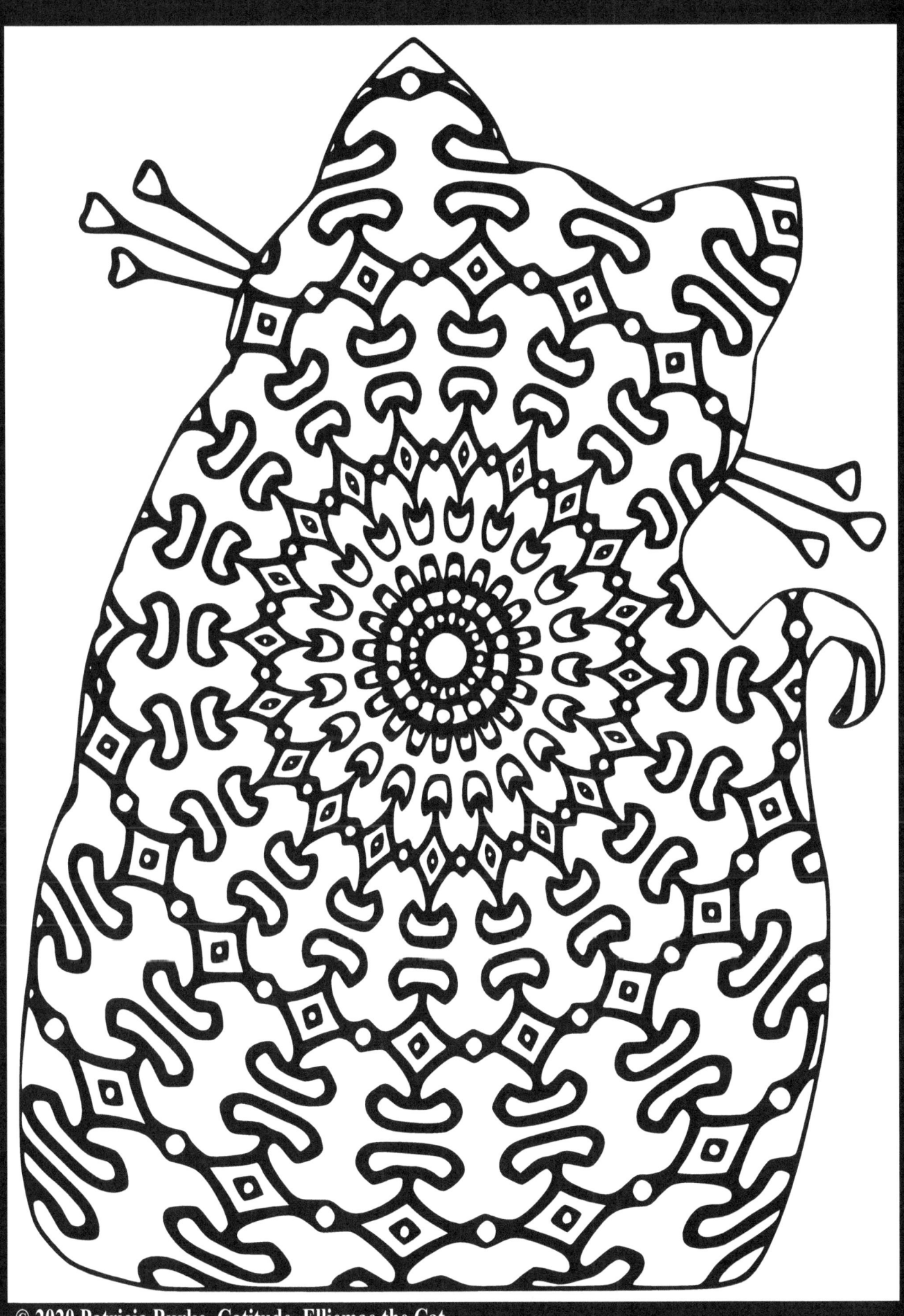

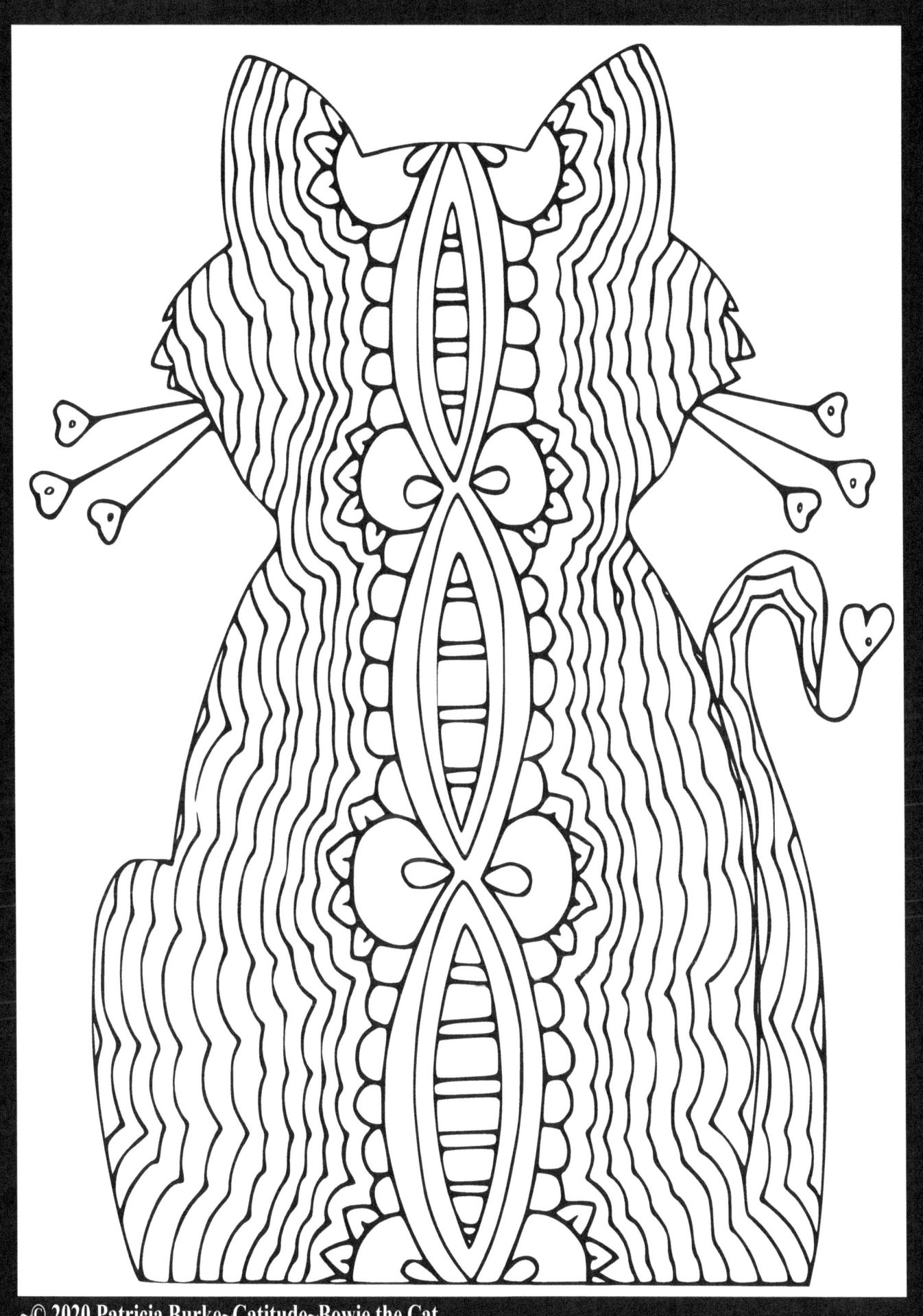

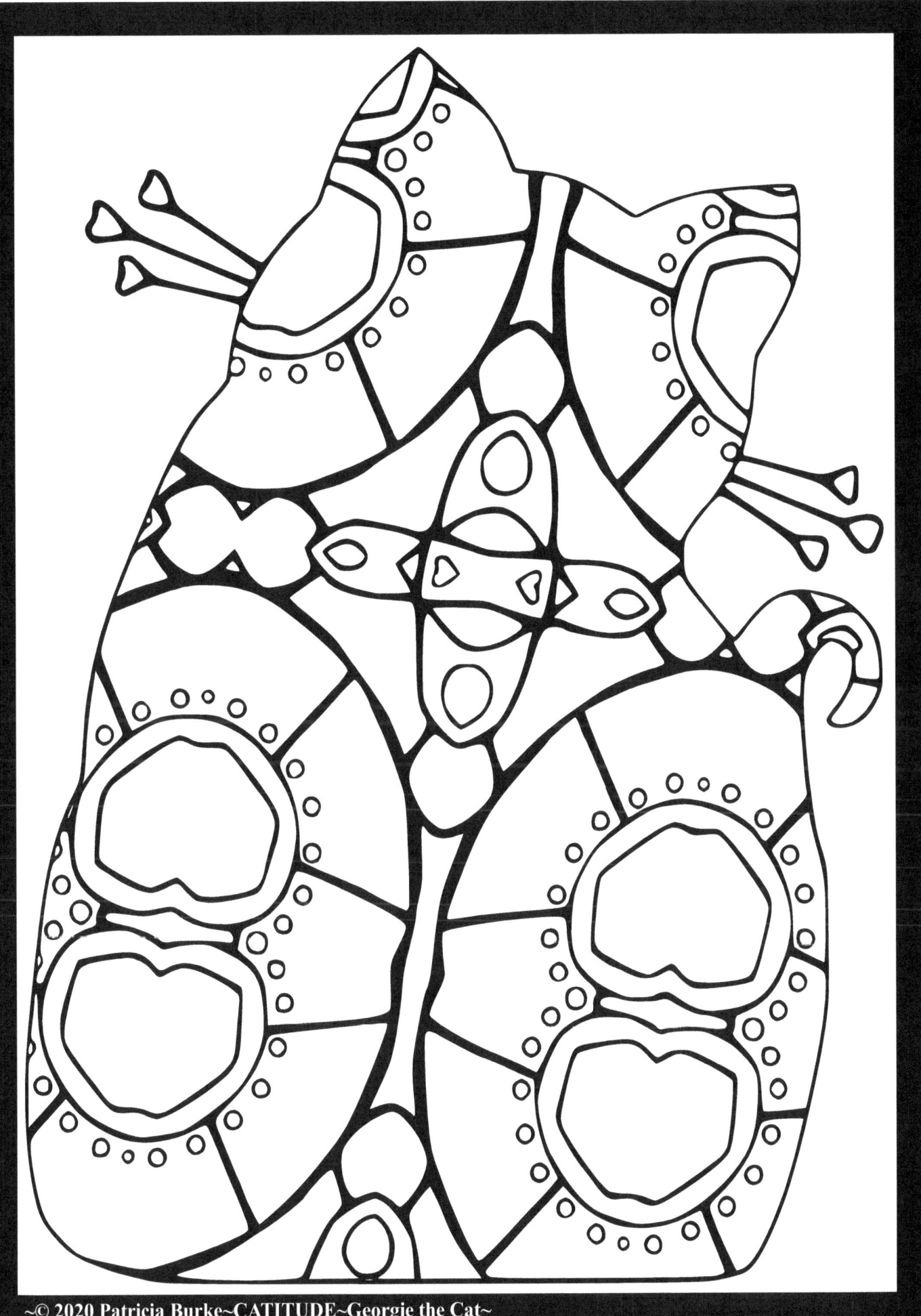

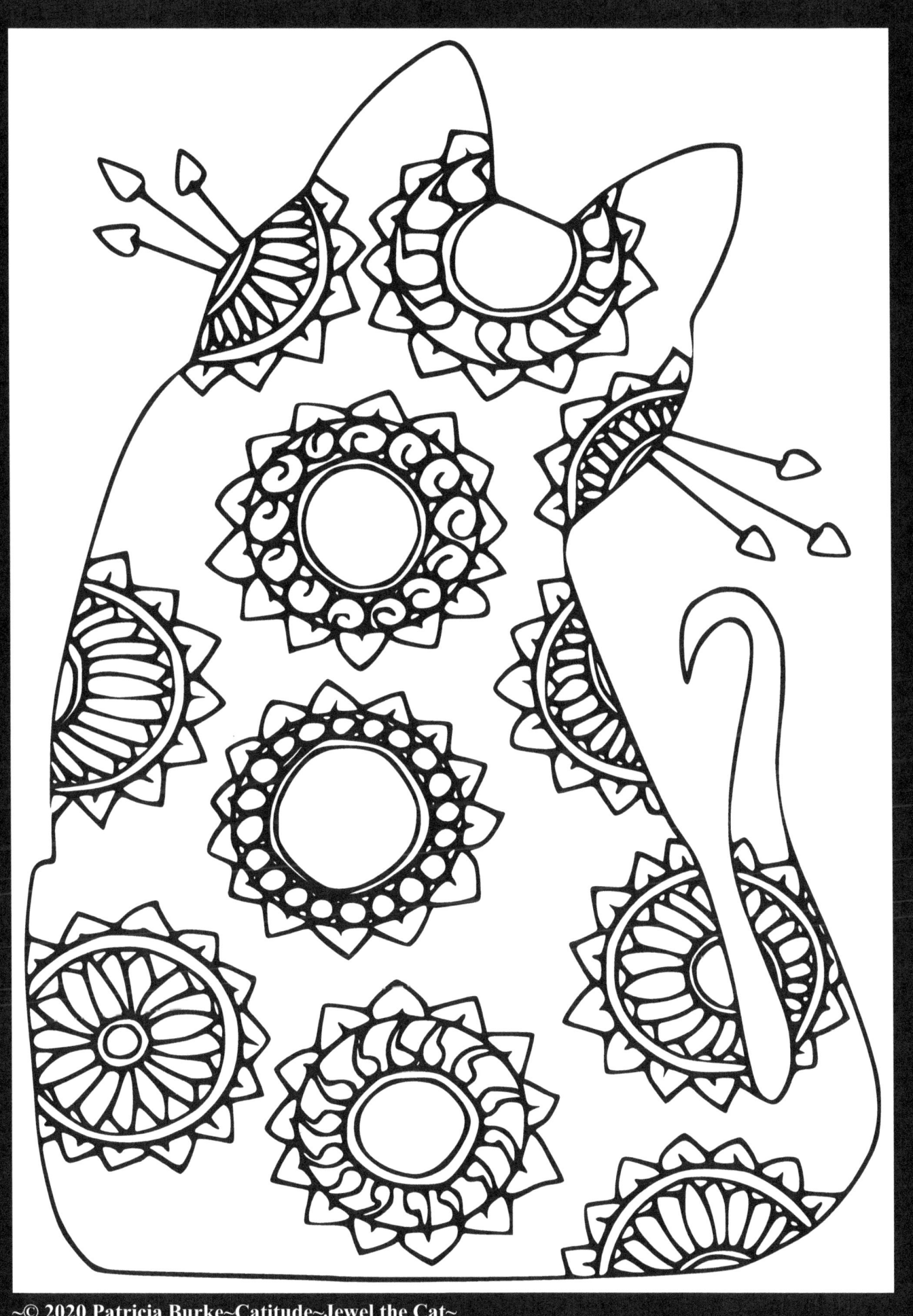

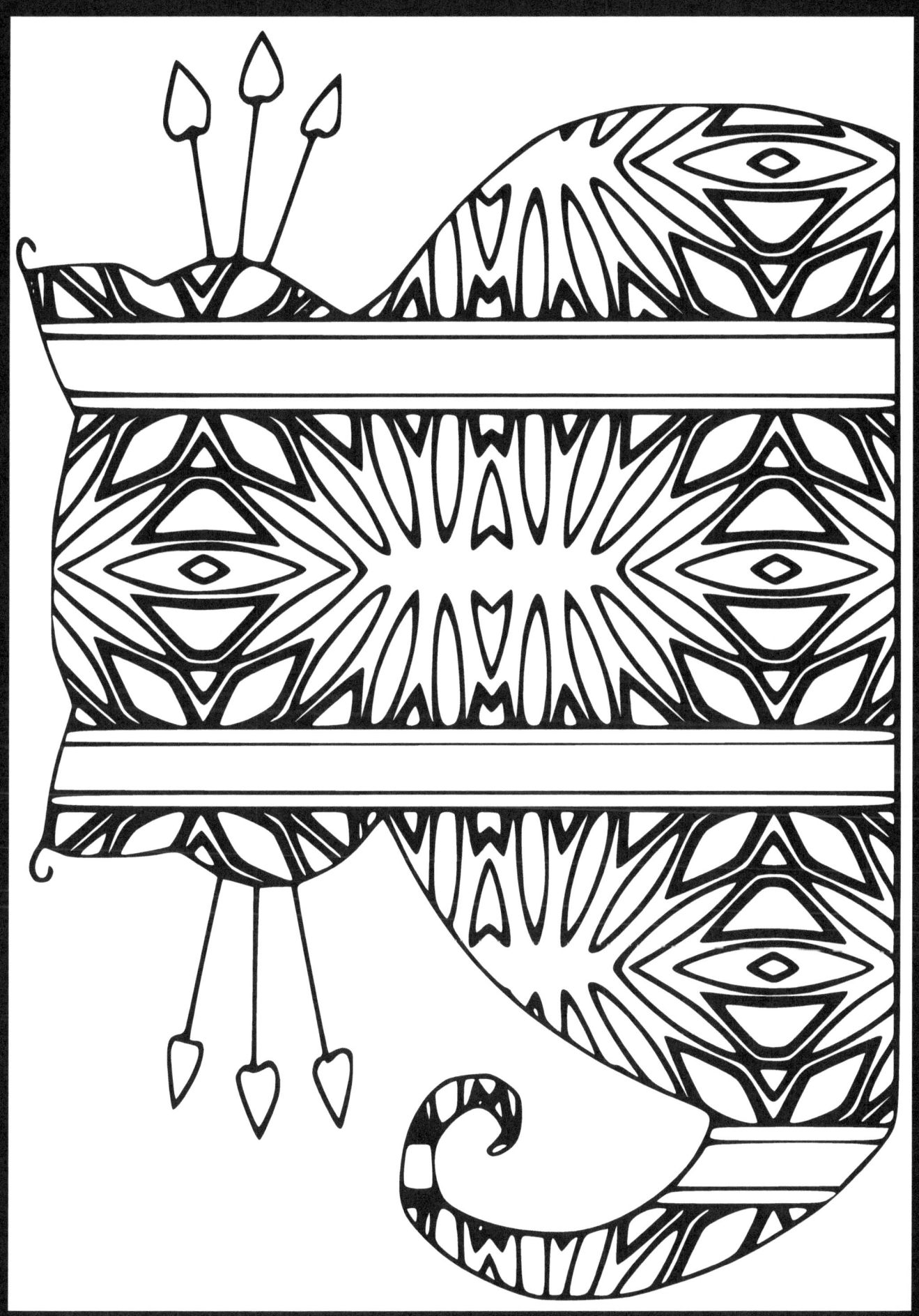

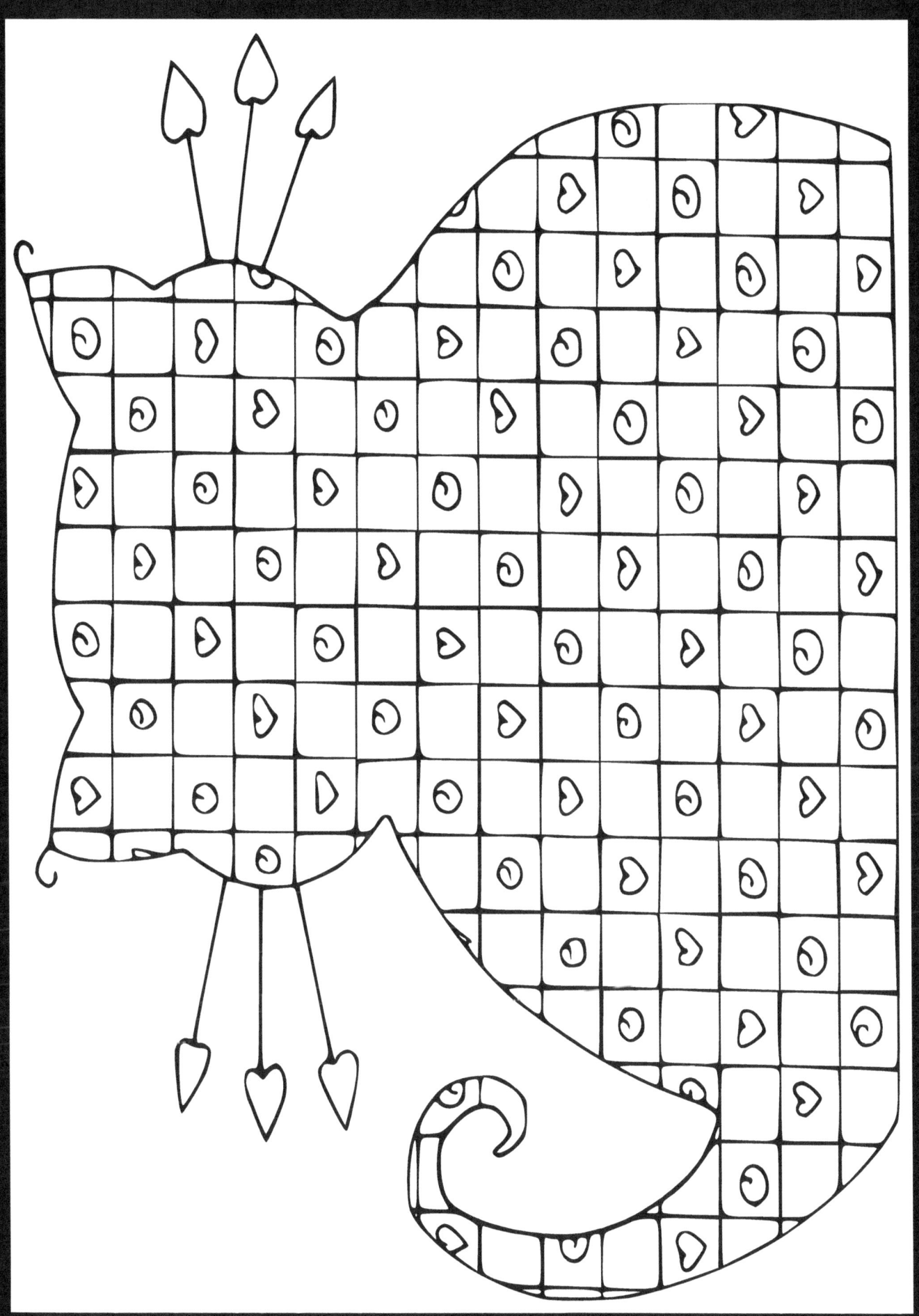

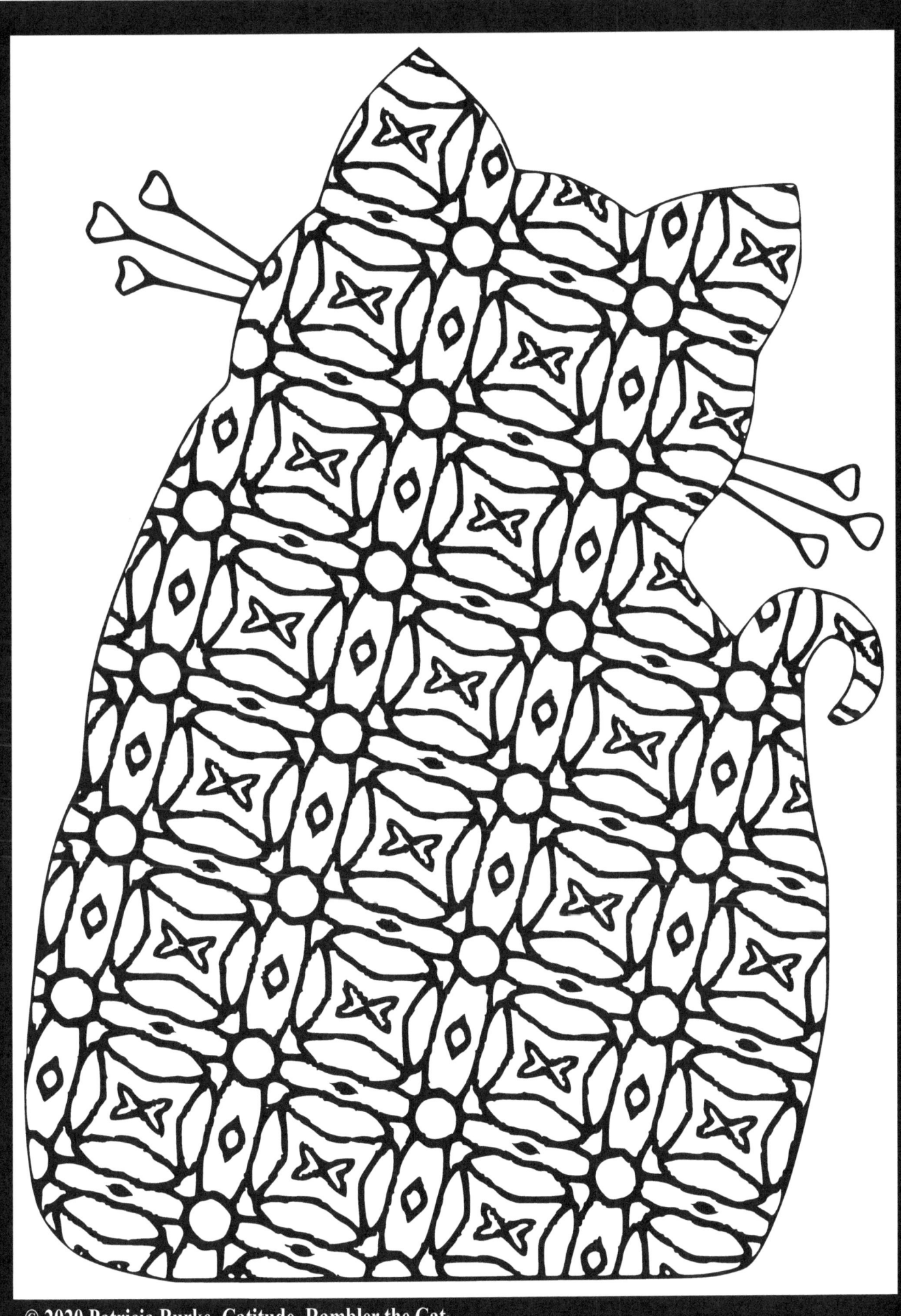

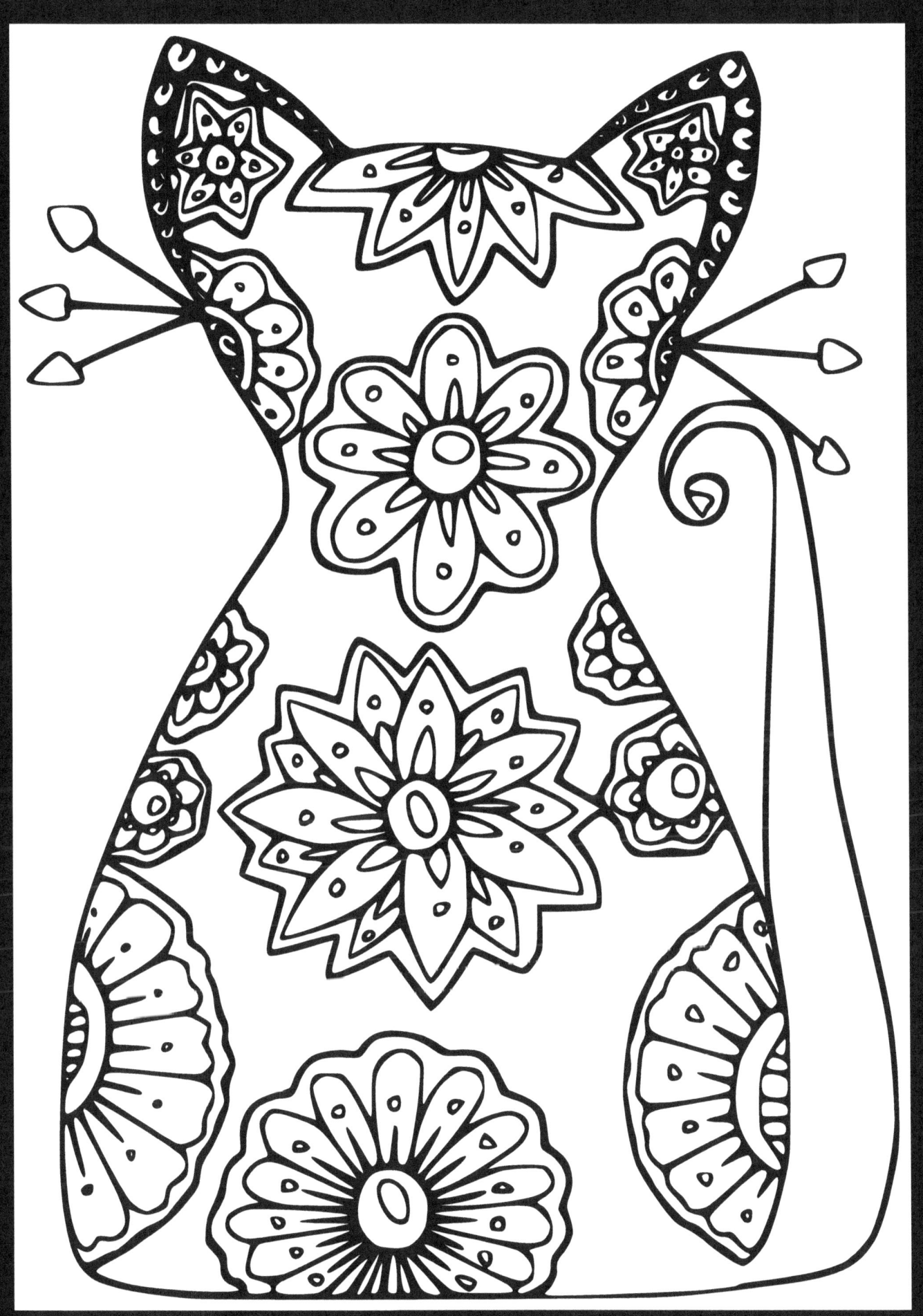

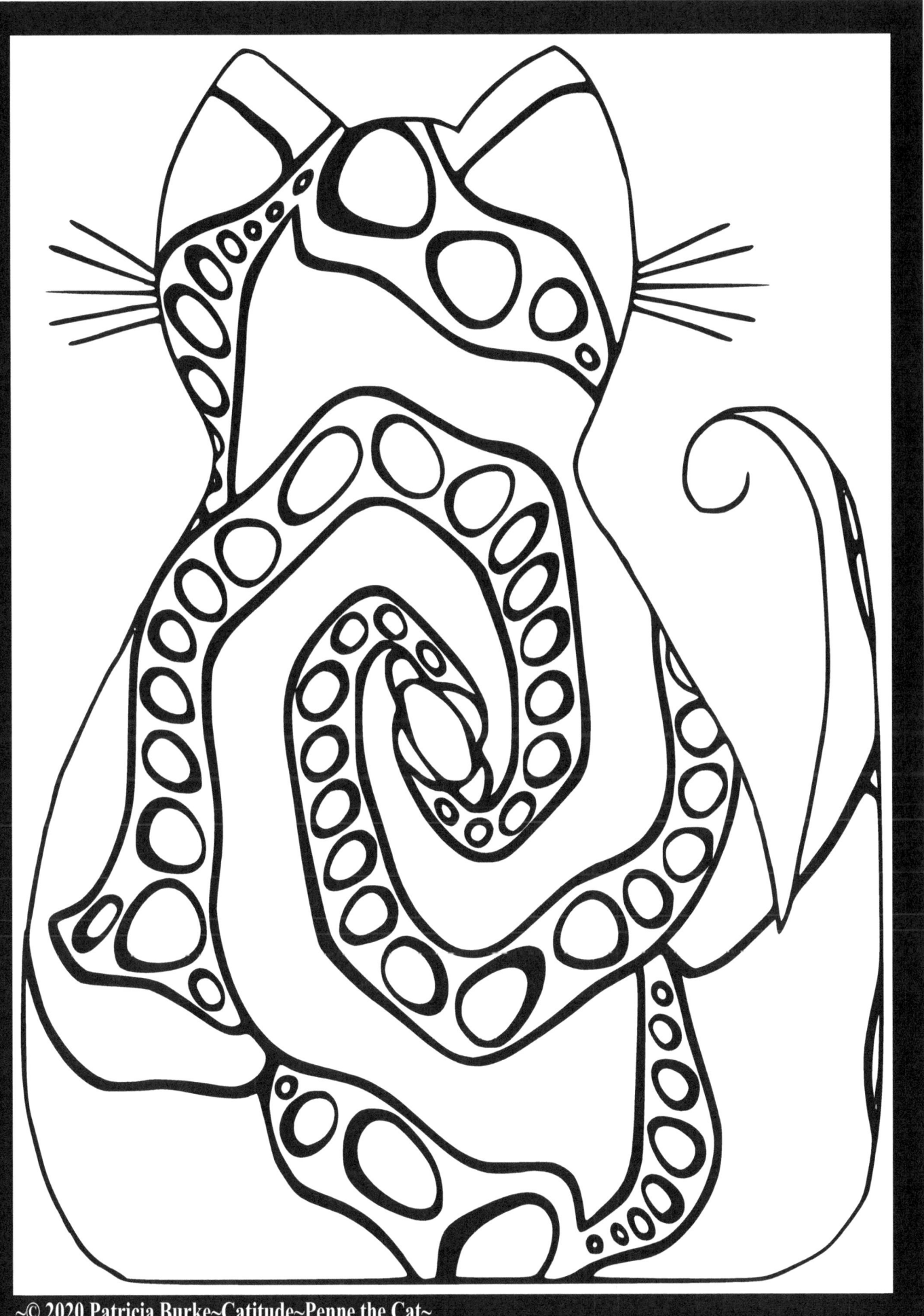

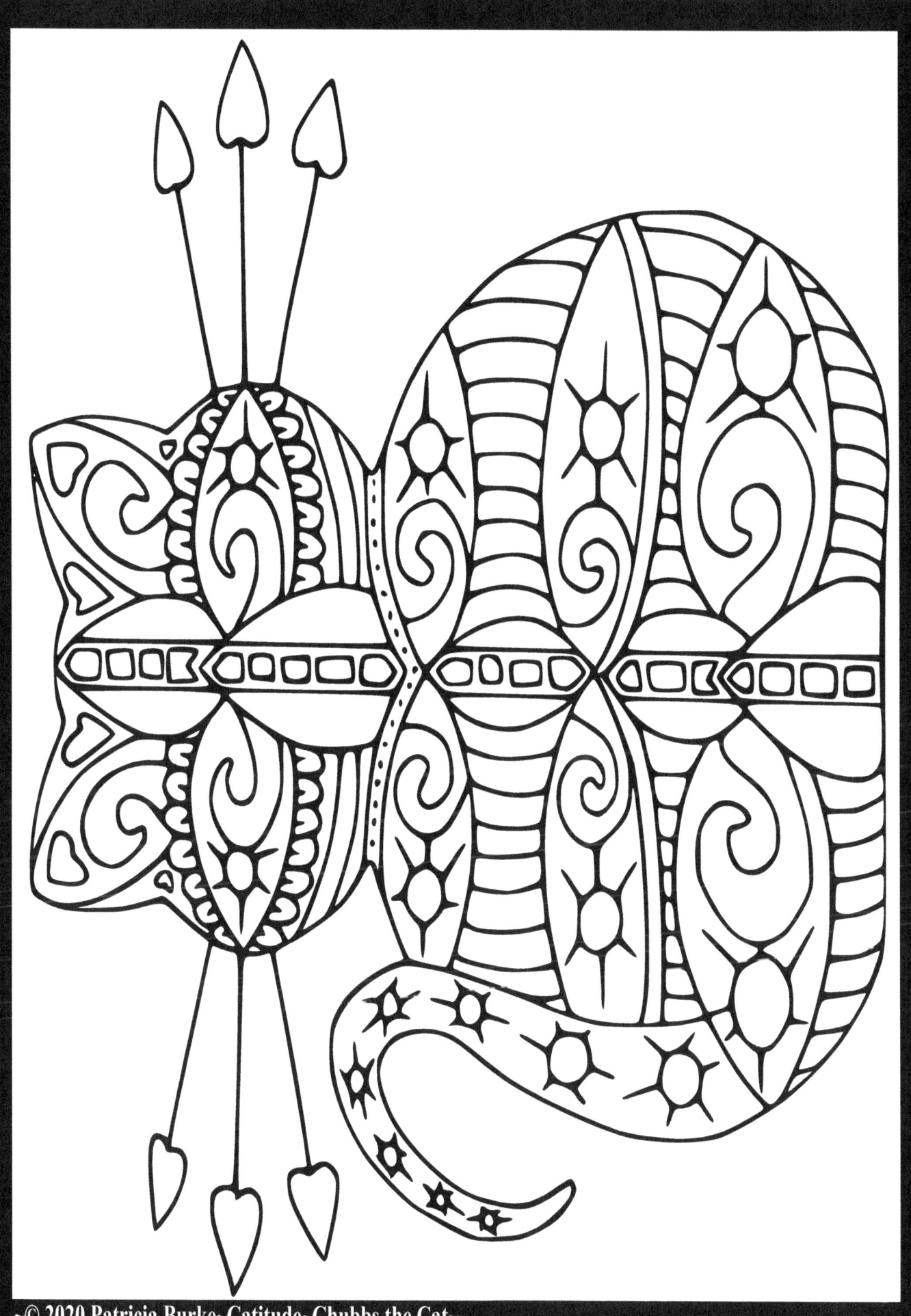

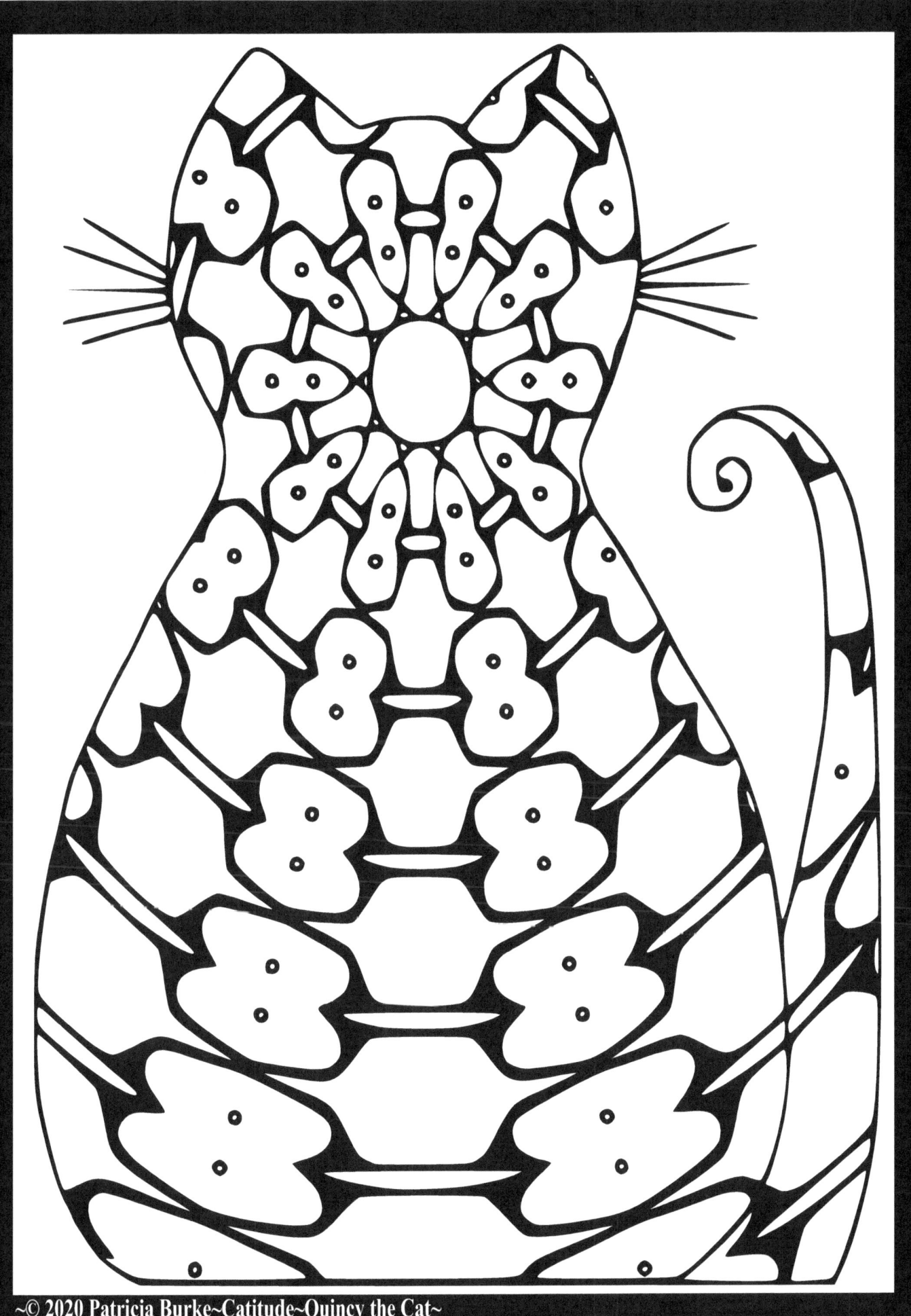

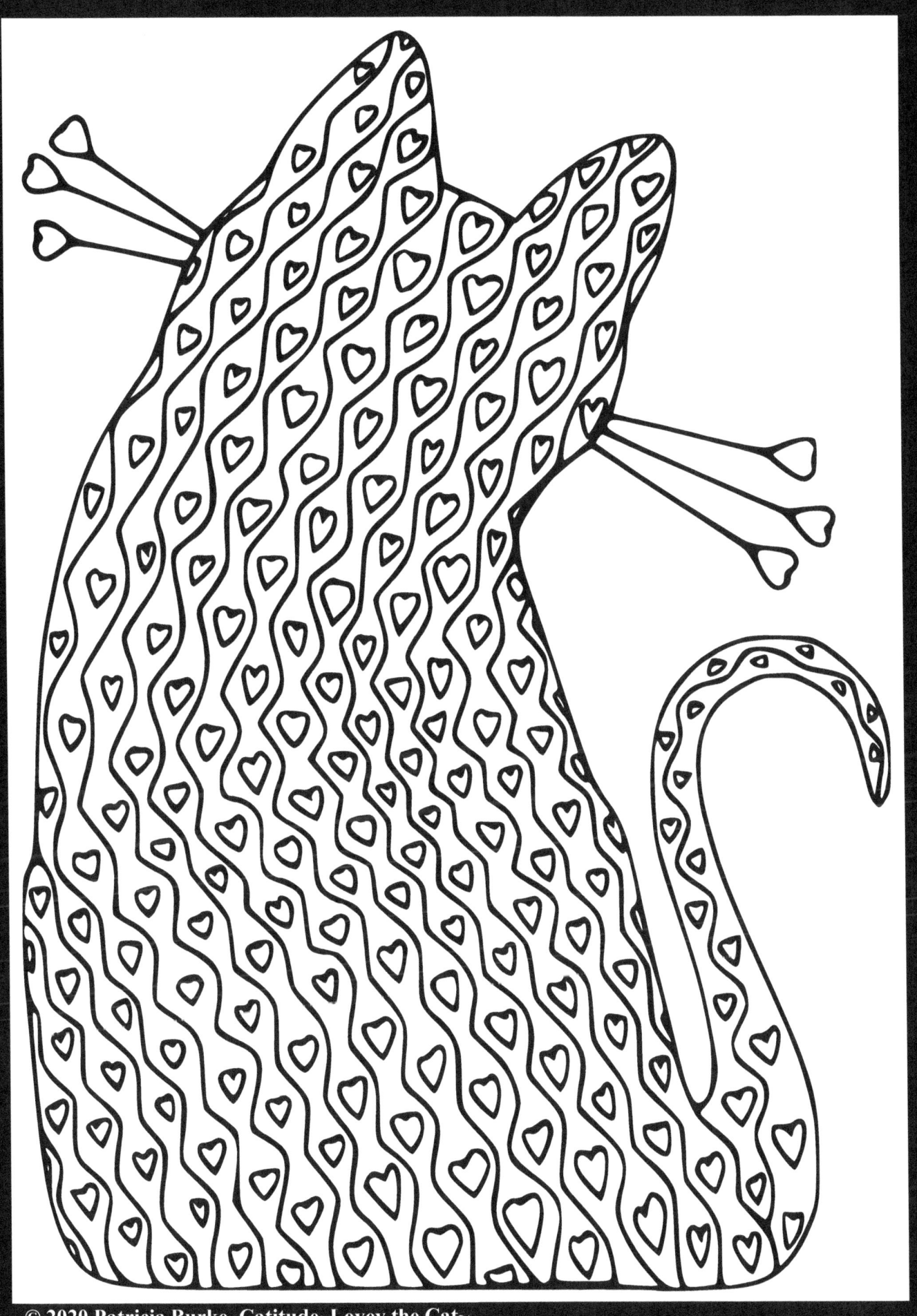

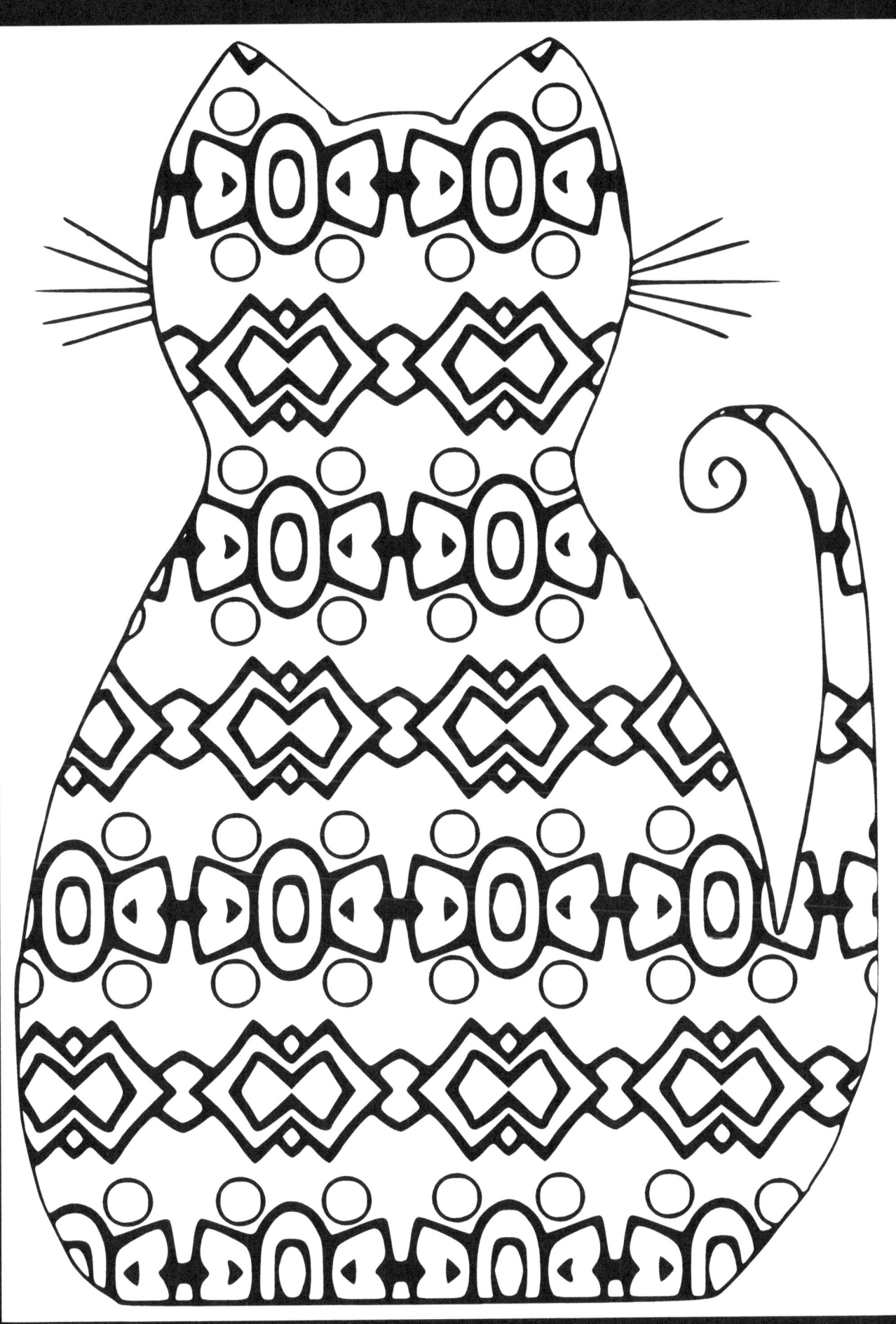

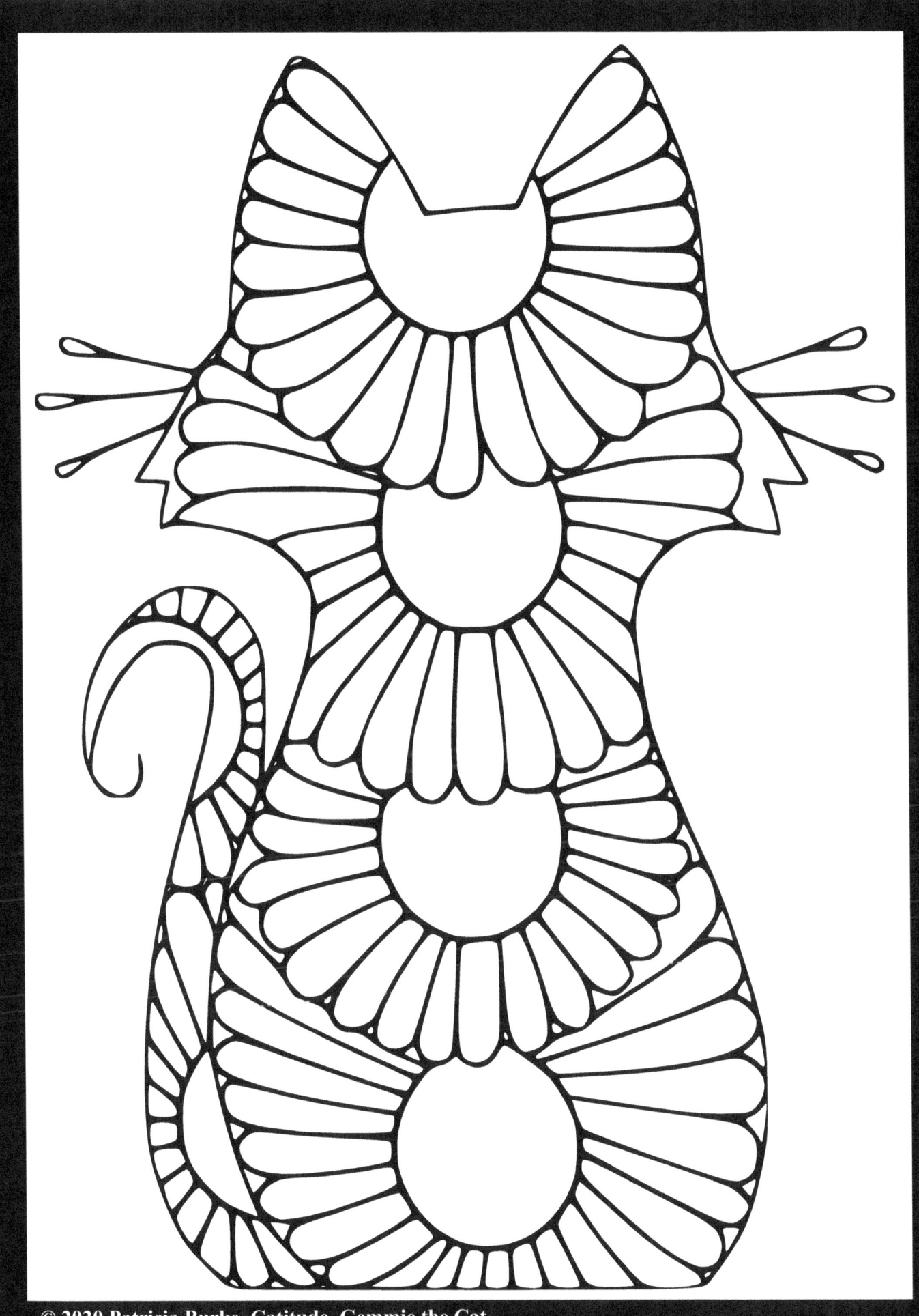

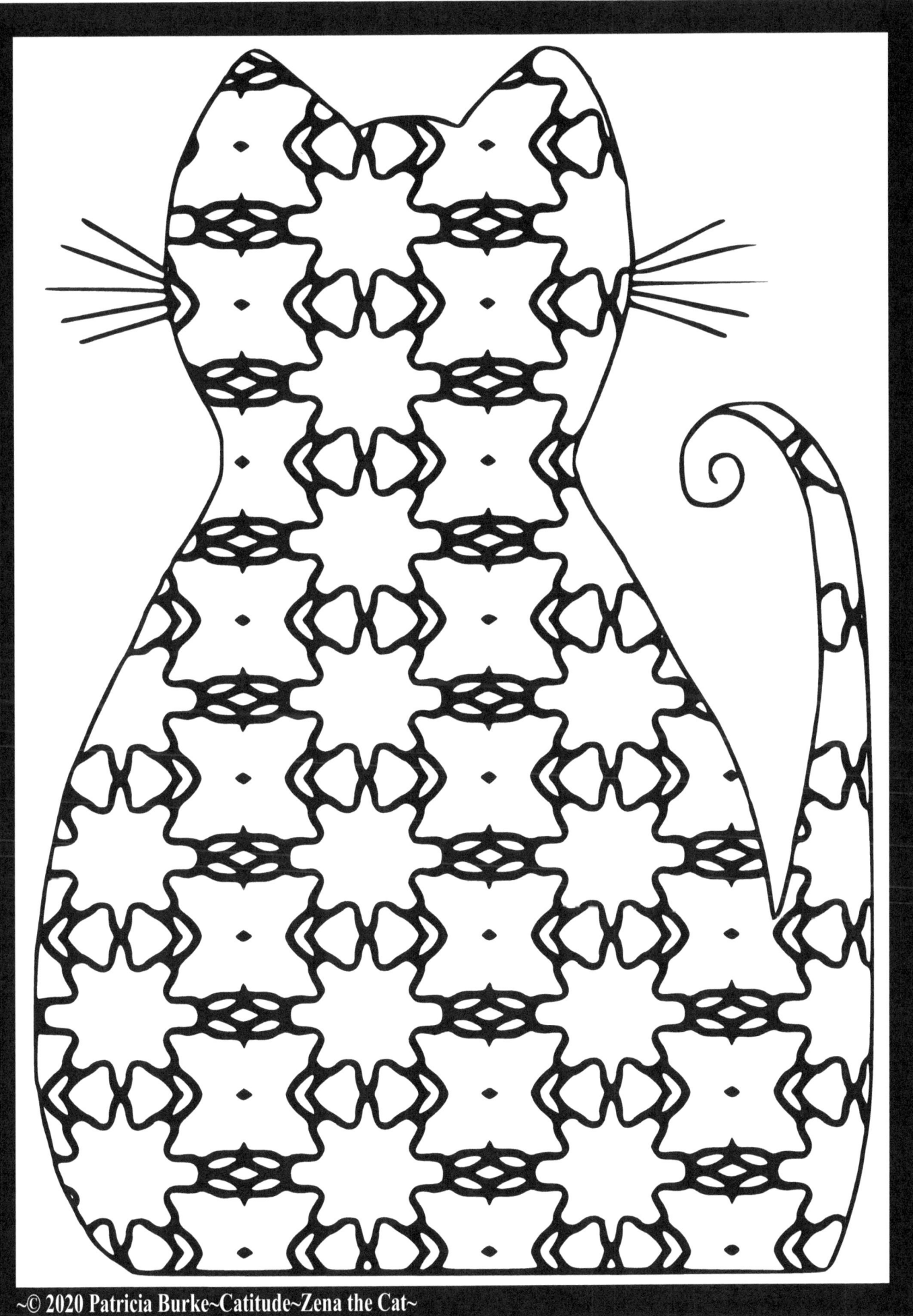

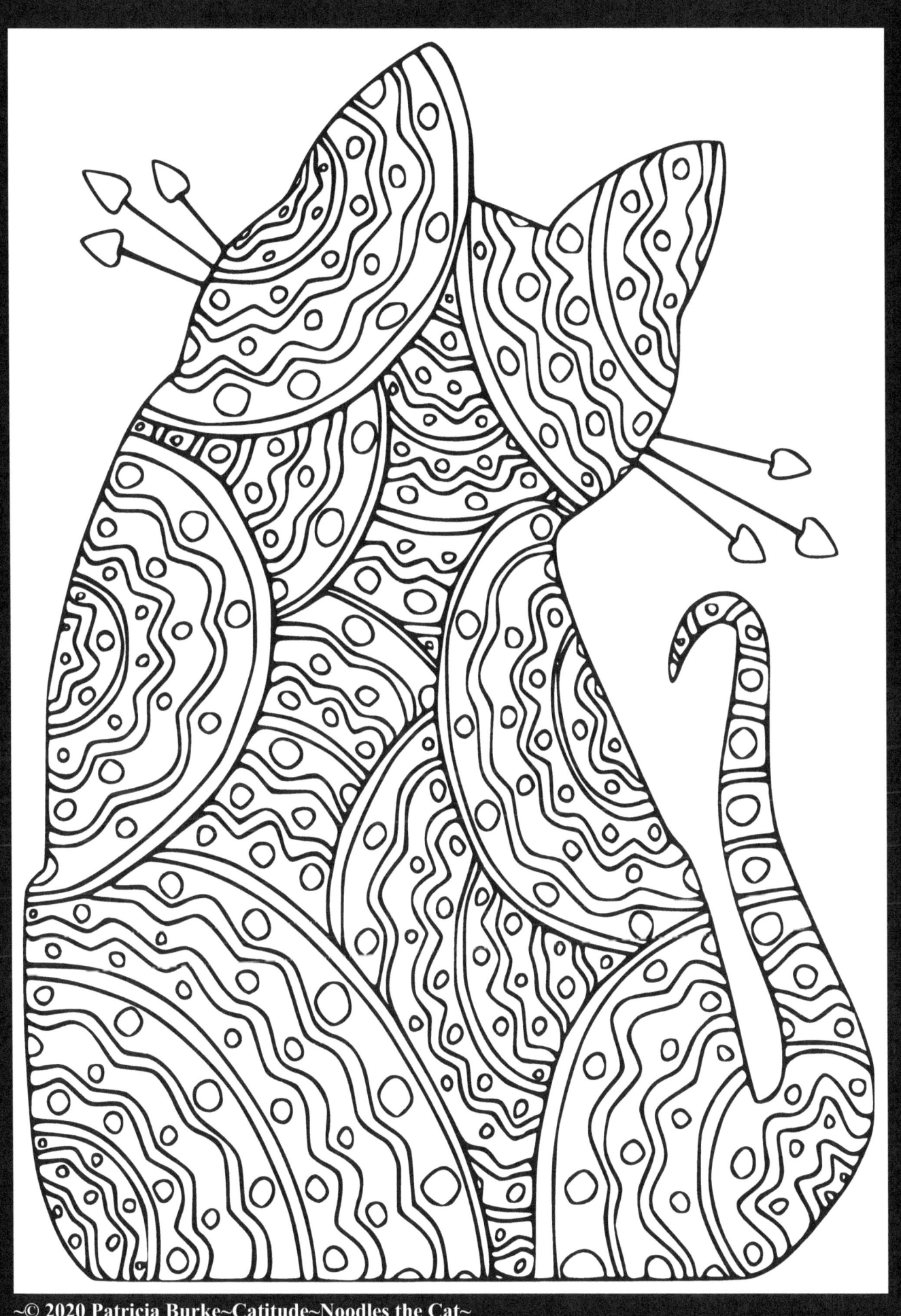

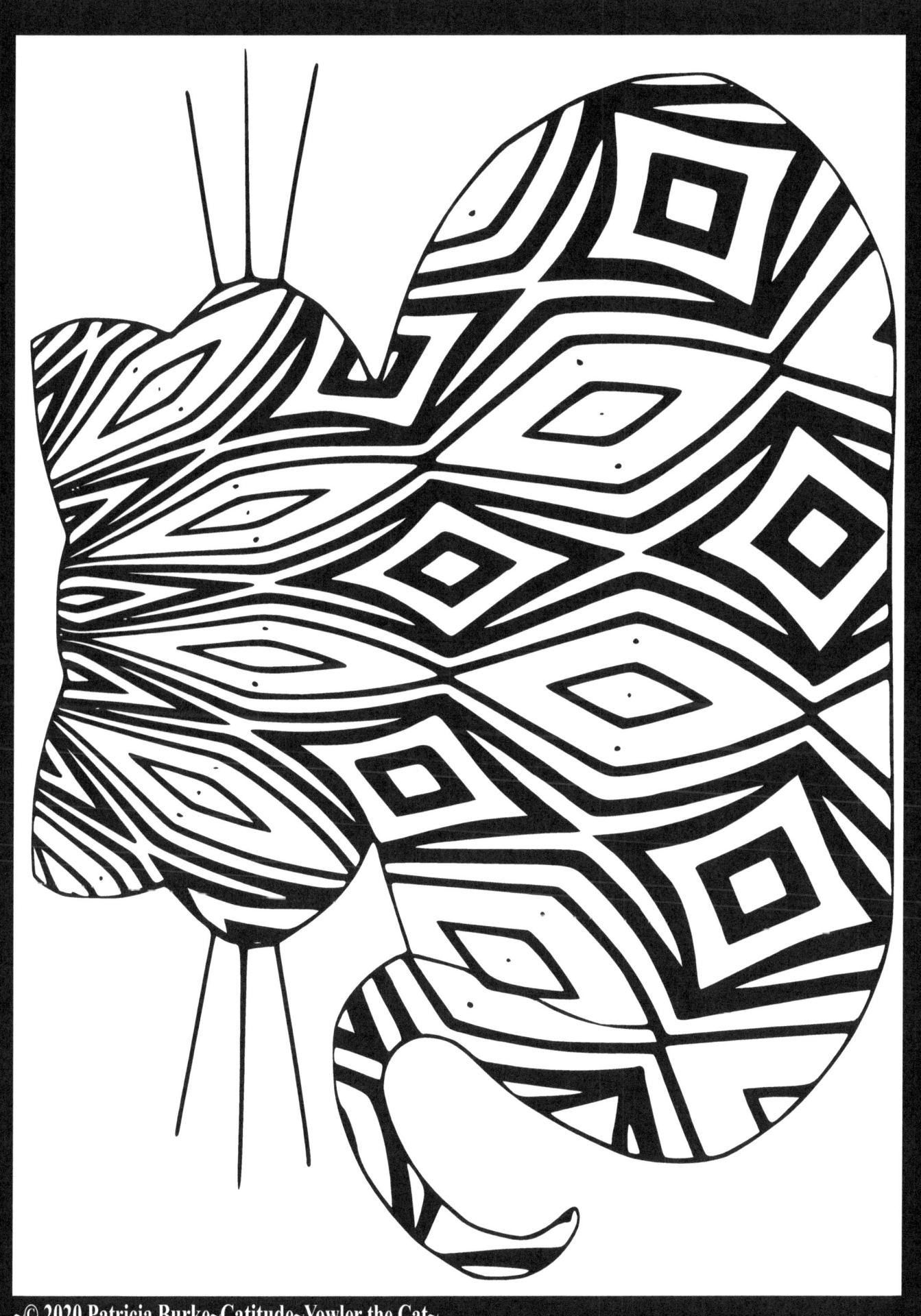

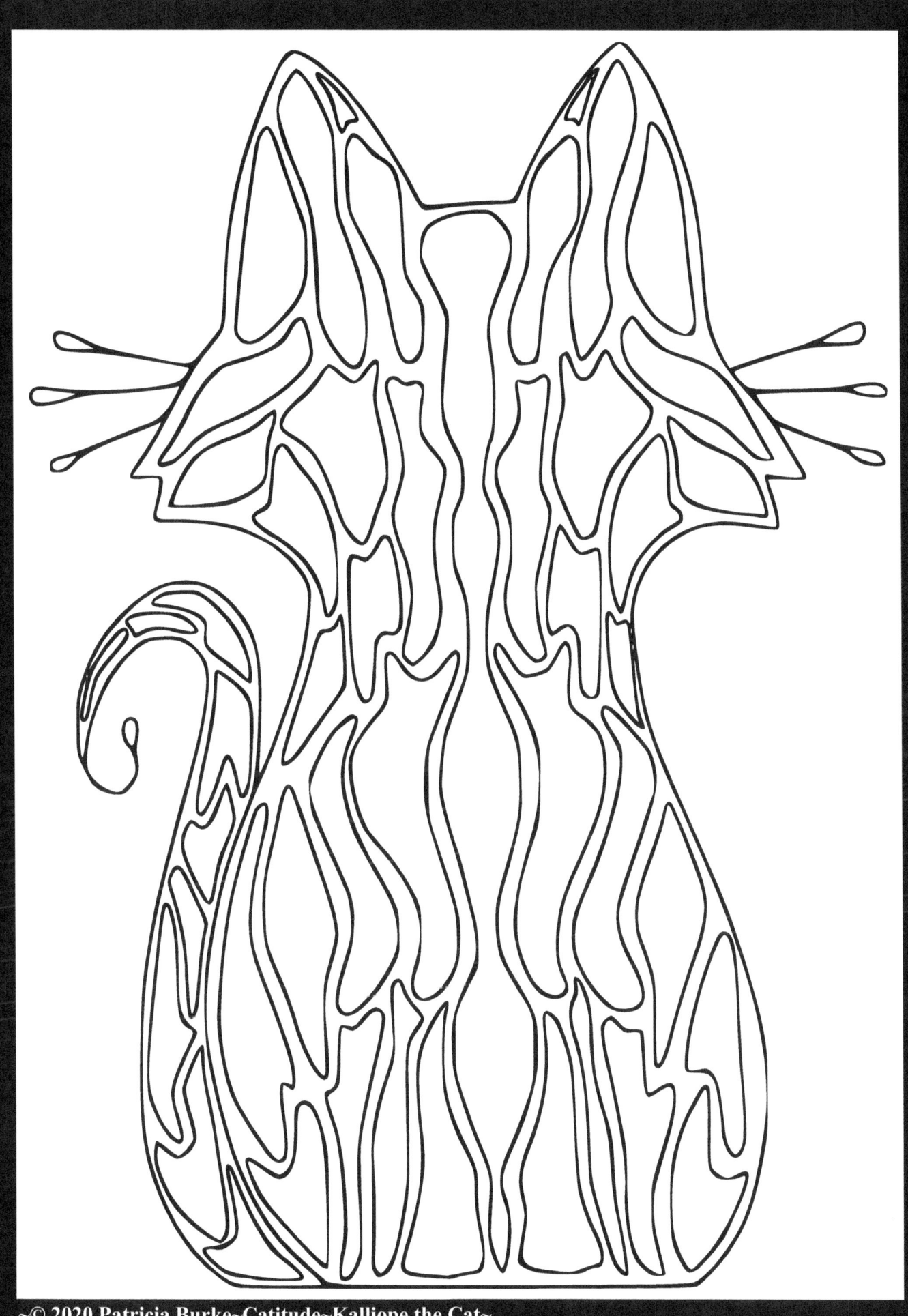

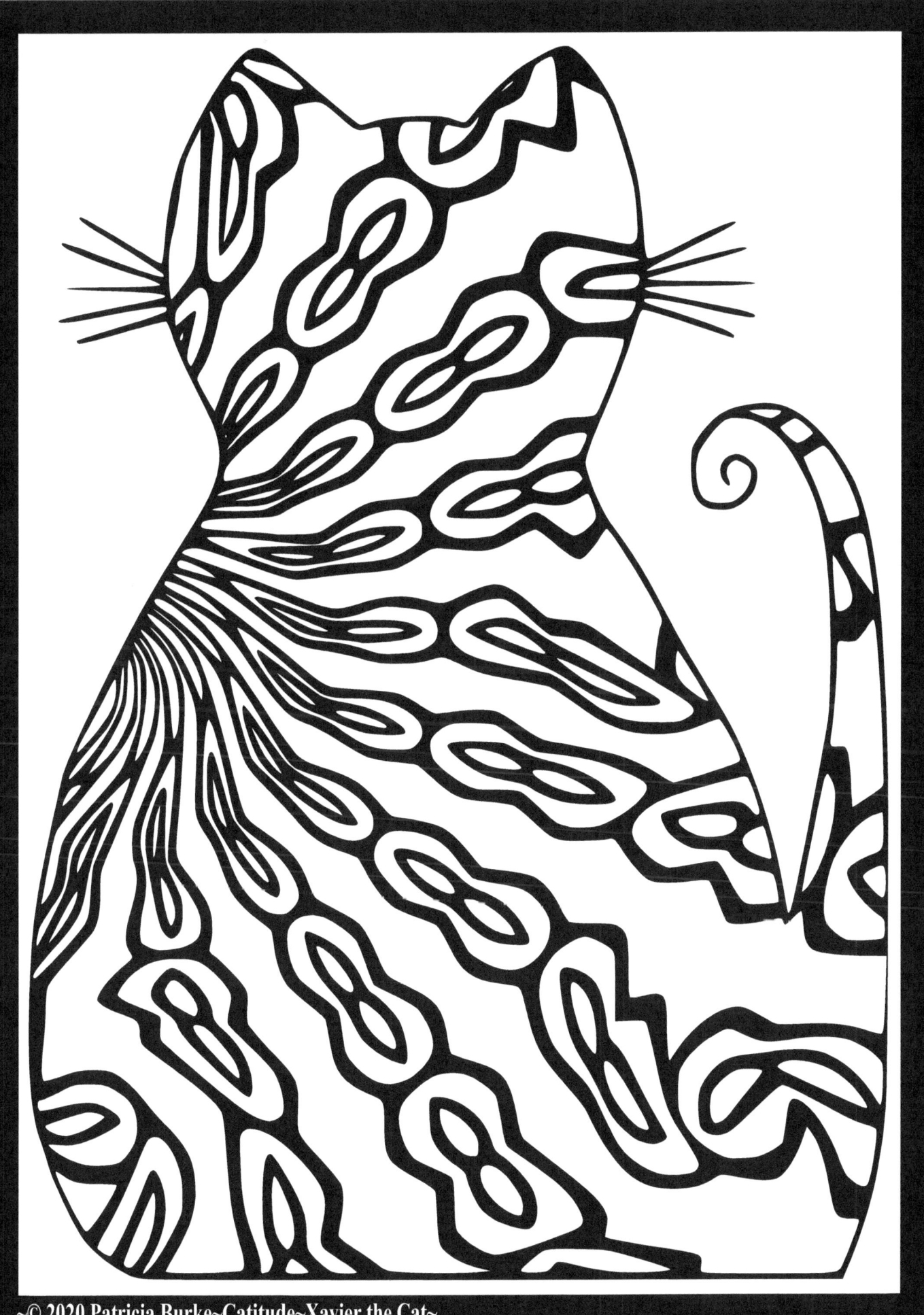

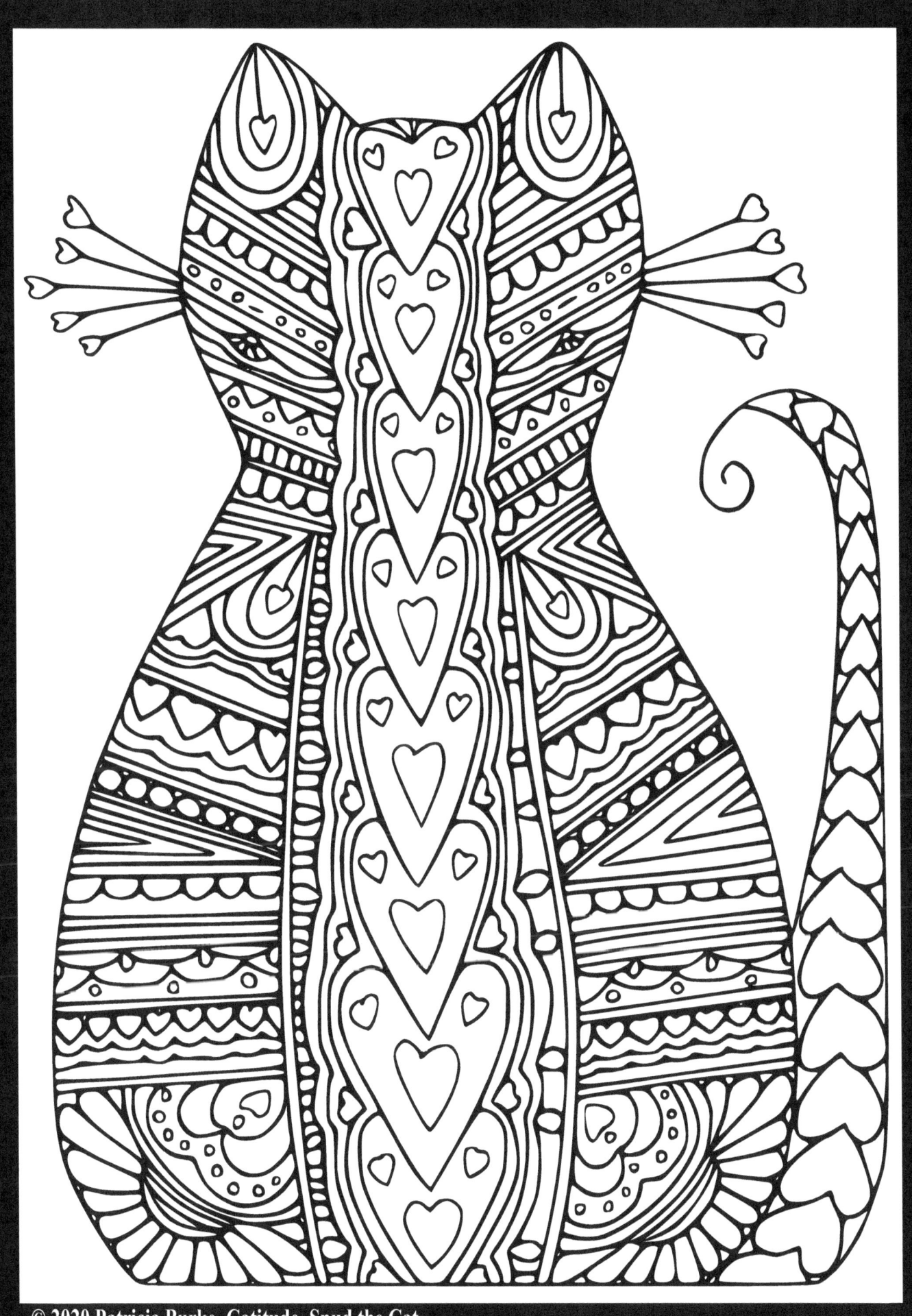

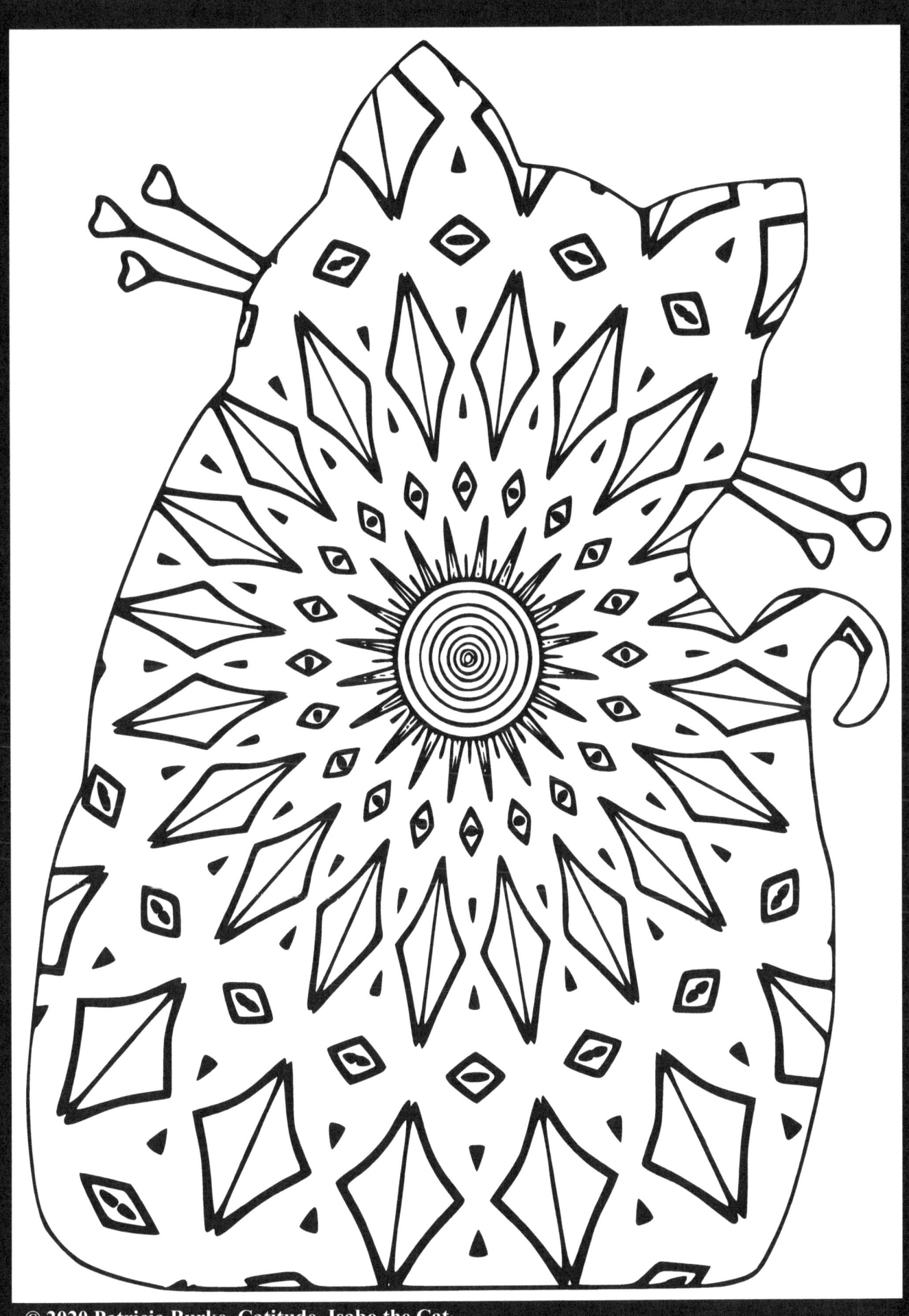

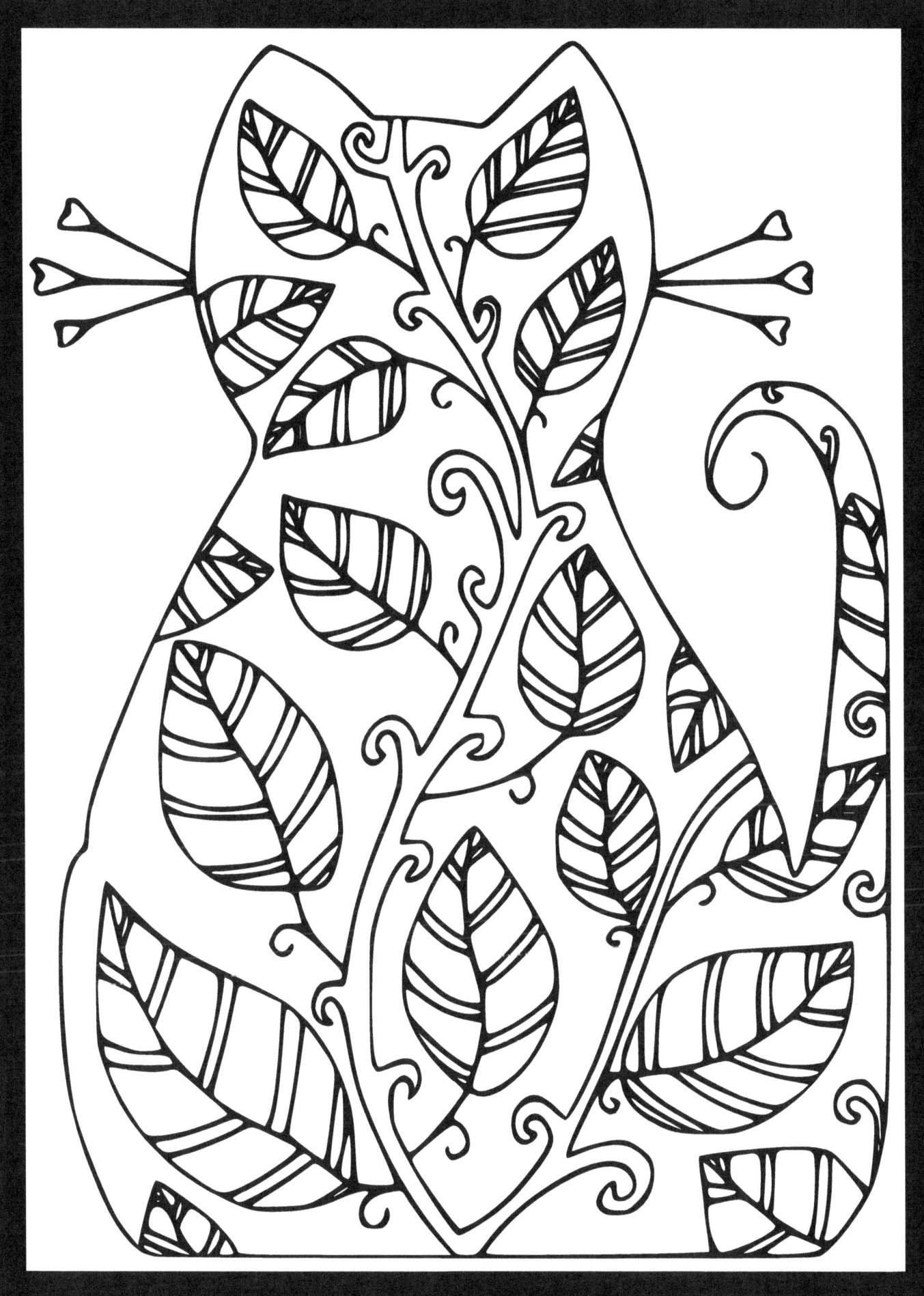

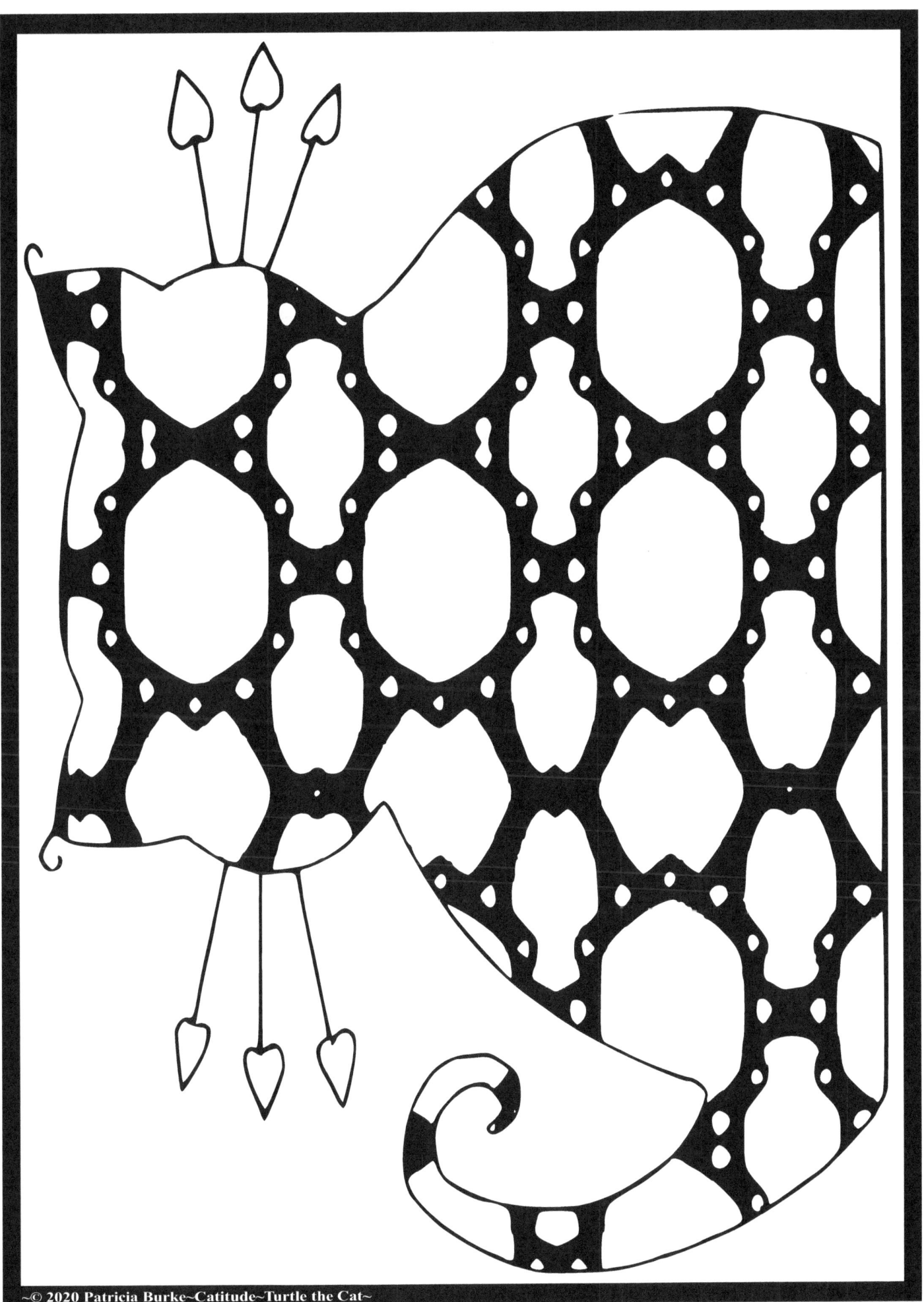

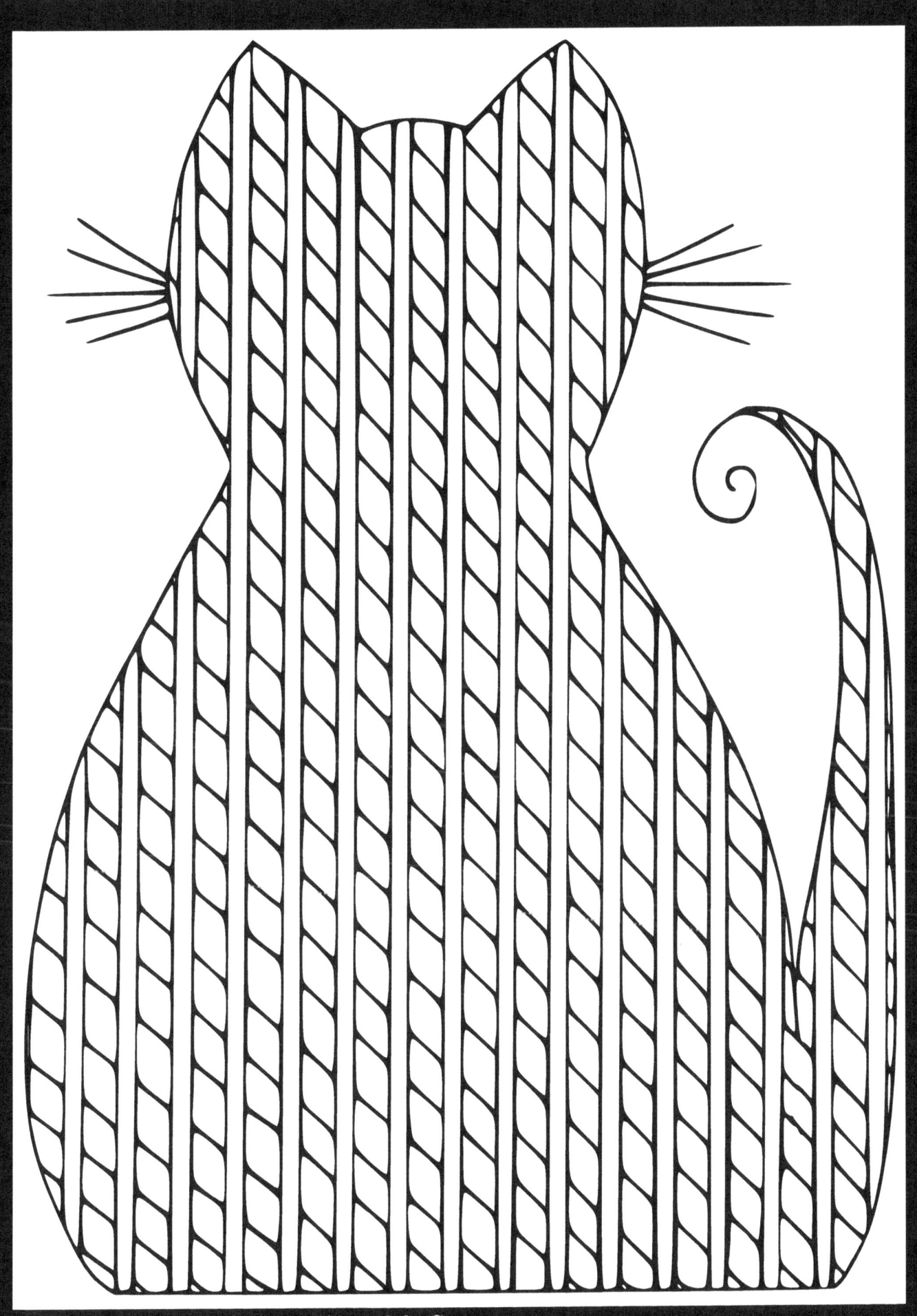

~© 2020 Patricia Burke~Catitude~Diamond the Cat~

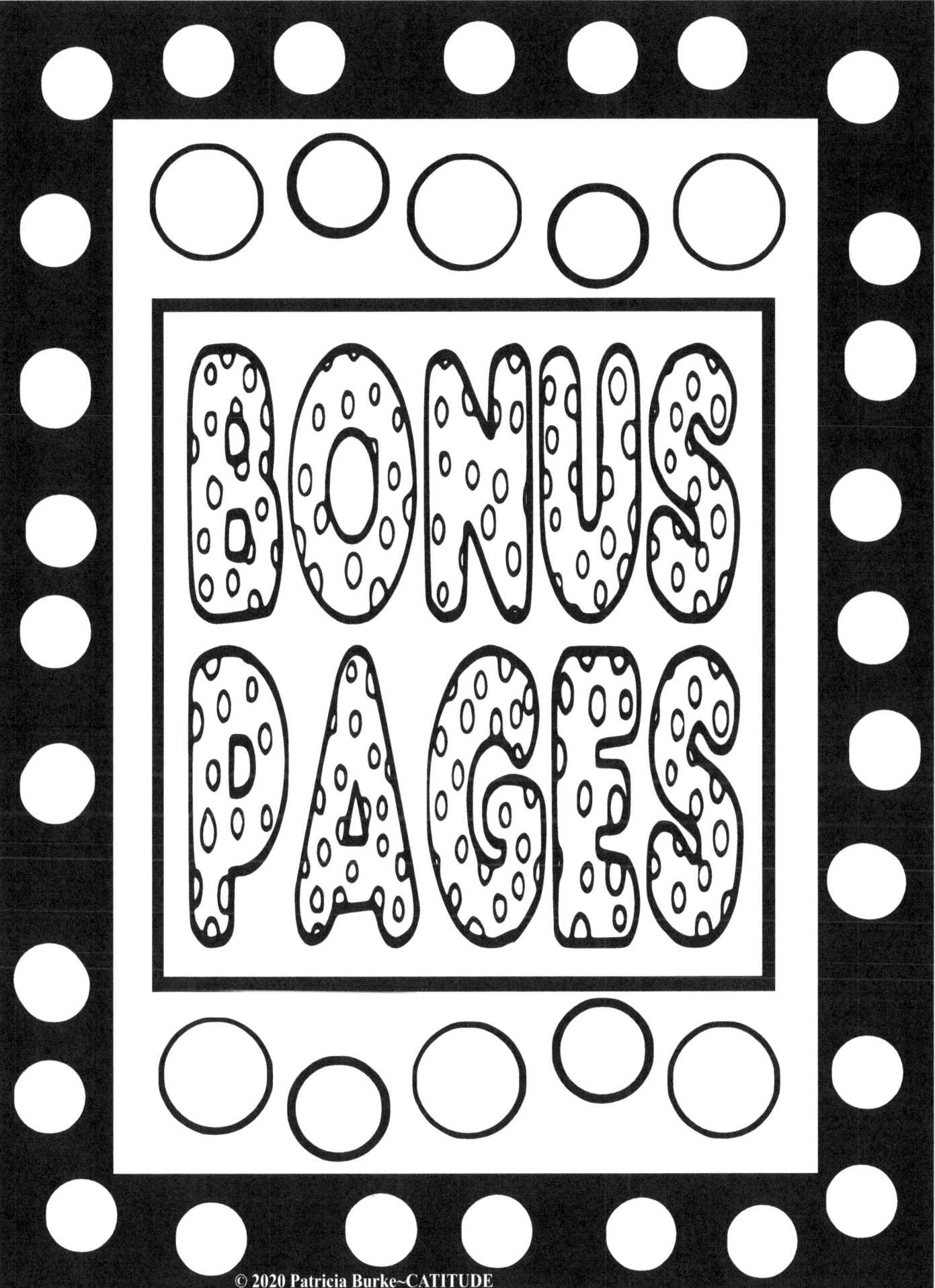

BONUS PAGES

CHUBBY DOTTY font~ courtesy of 1001fonts.com

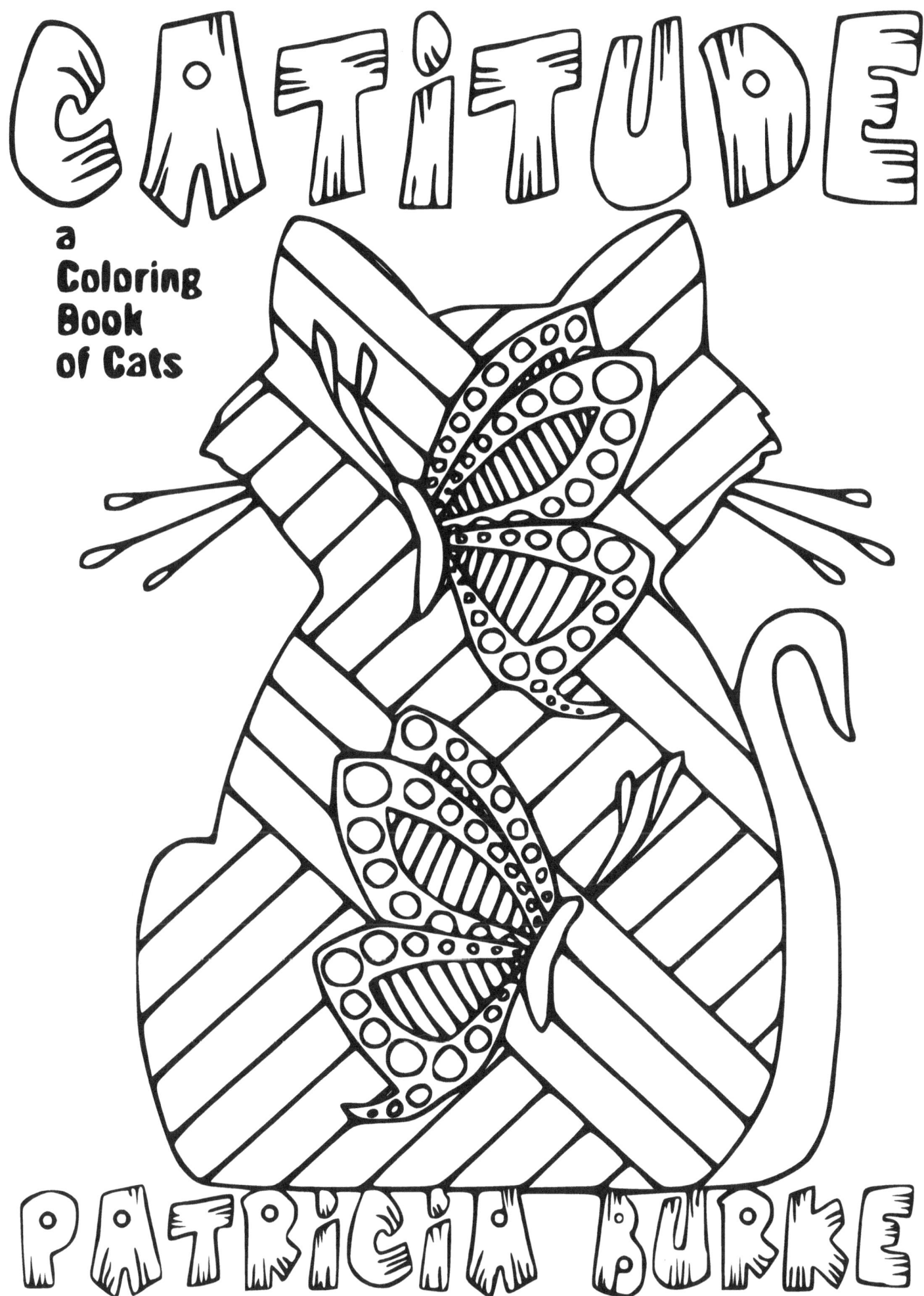

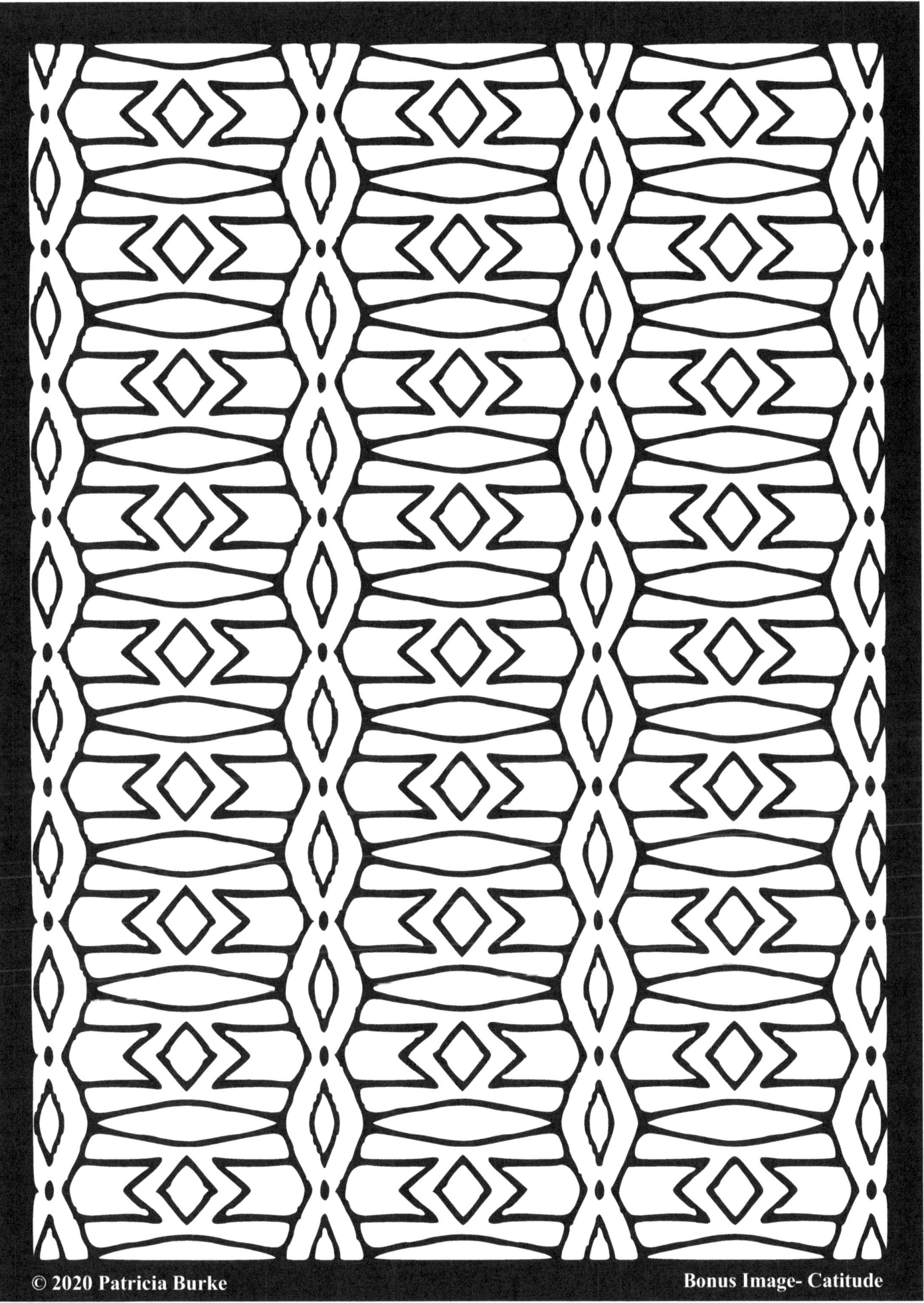

© 2020 Patricia Burke

Bonus Image- Catitude

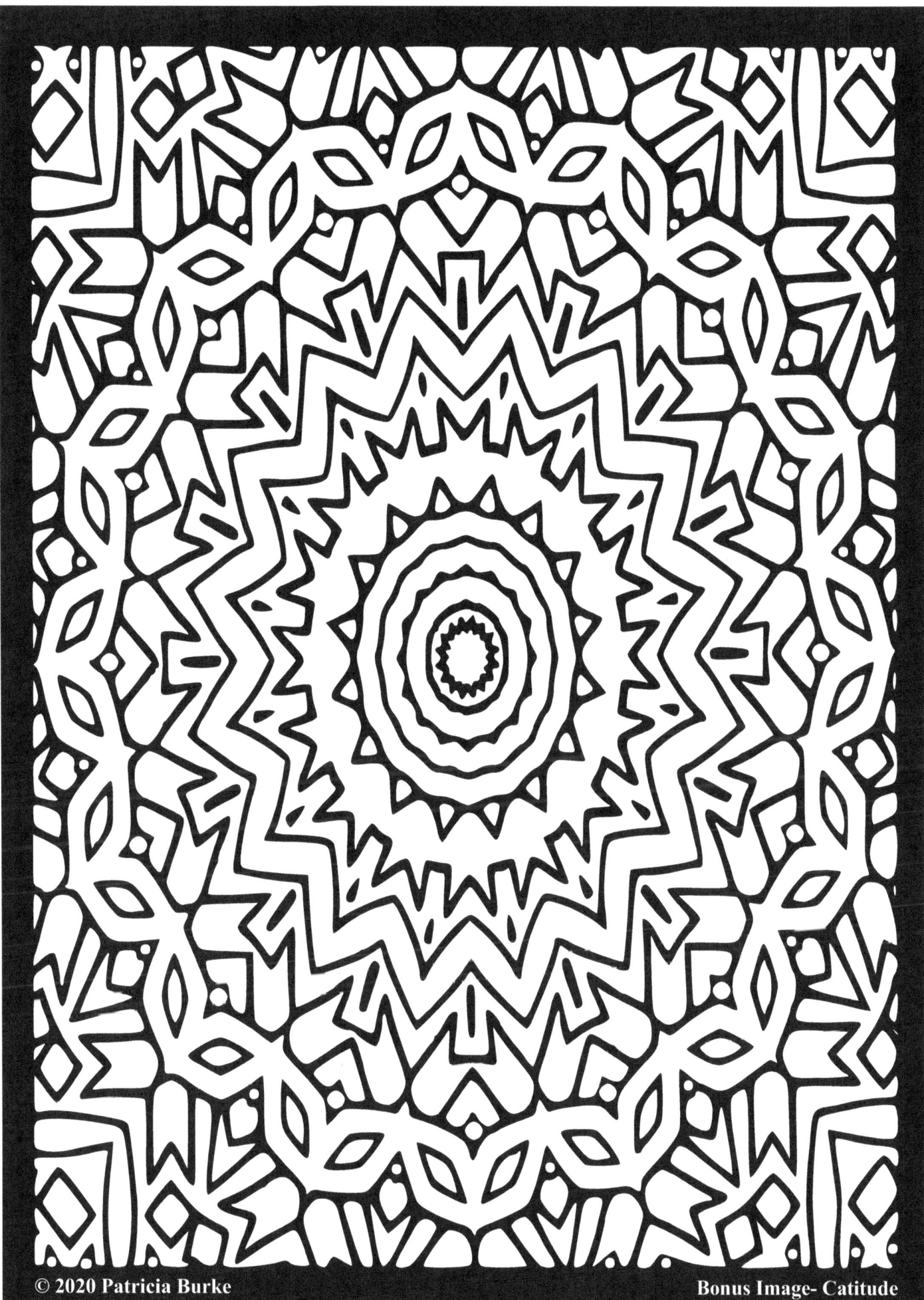

© 2020 Patricia Burke

Bonus Image- Catitude

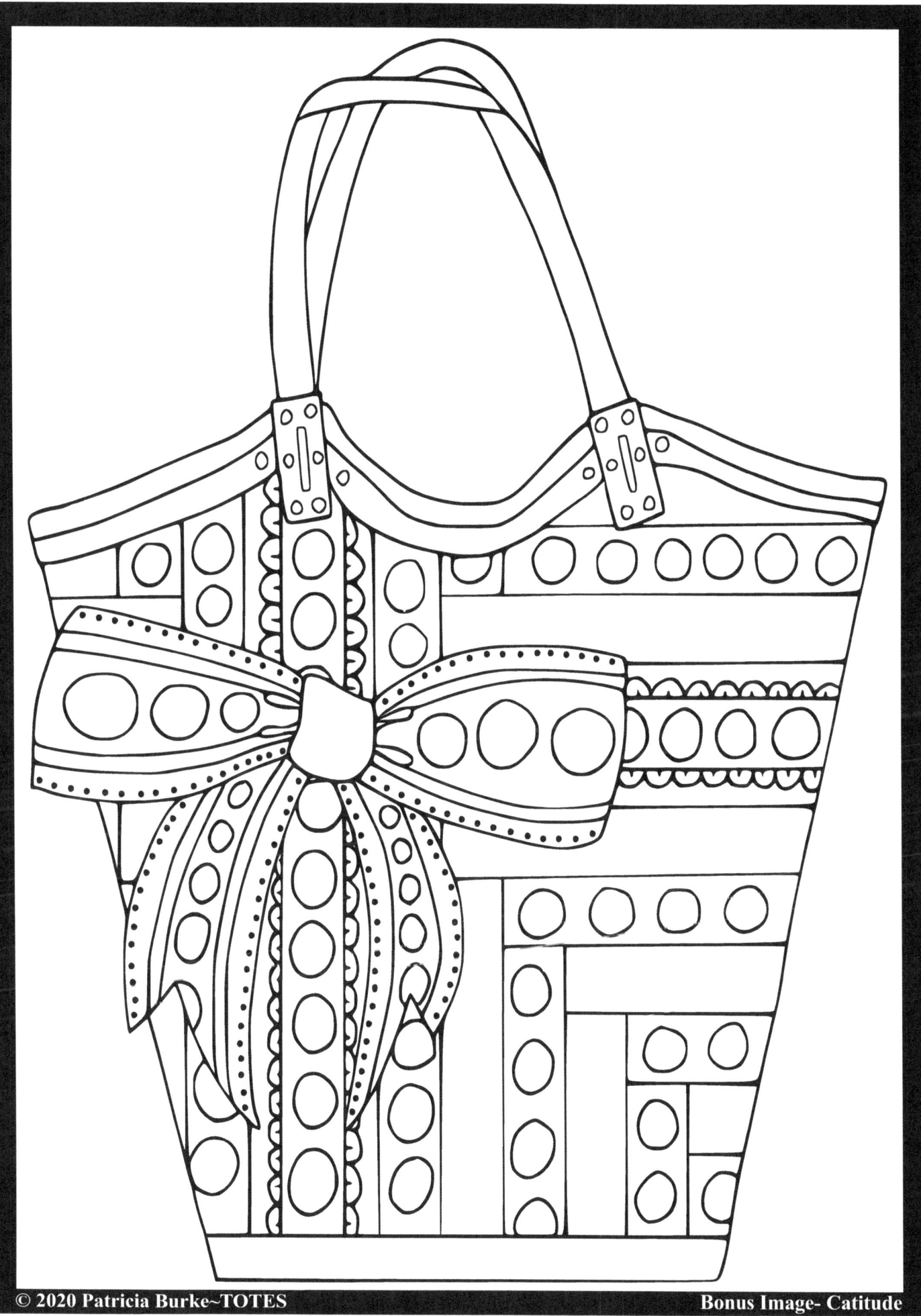

Bonus Image- Catitude

BLOTTER PAGE

BLOTTER PAGE

BLOTTER PAGE

www.ingramcontent.com/pod-product-compliance
Lightning Source LLC
Chambersburg PA
CBHW081736220526

45468CB00008B/2126